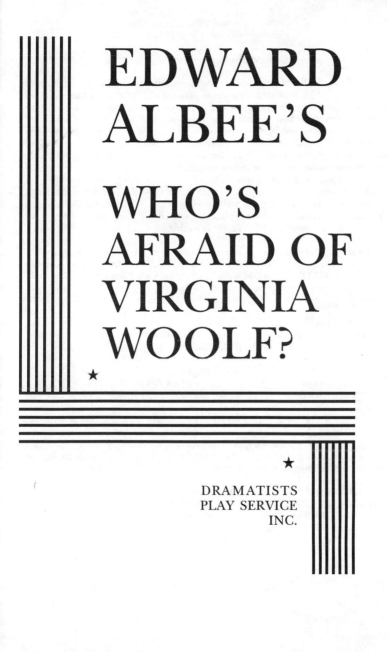

EDWARD ALBEE'S

WHO'S AFRAID OF VIRGINIA WOOLF?

★

DRAMATISTS
PLAY SERVICE
INC.

WHO'S AFRAID OF VIRGINIA WOOLF was first presented by Theater 1963 (Richard Barr and Clinton Wilder) at the Billy Rose Theatre, in New York City, on October 13, 1962. It was directed by Alan Schneider; and the production was designed by William Ritman. The cast, in order of appearance, was as follows:

MARTHA .... Uta Hagen

GEORGE .... Arthur Hill

HONEY .... Melinda Dillon

NICK .... George Grizzard

ACT ONE
FUN AND GAMES

ACT TWO
WALPURGISNACHT

ACT THREE
THE EXORCISM

THE PLAYERS

MARTHA
A large, boisterous woman, 52, looking somewhat younger. Ample, but not fleshy.

GEORGE
Her husband, 46. Thin; hair going gray.

HONEY
26, a petite blond girl, rather plain.

NICK
30, her husband. Blond, well put-together, good looking.

THE SCENE
The living room of a house on the campus of a small New England college.

4

Who's Afraid of
Virginia Woolf?

ACT ONE

FUN AND GAMES

Set in darkness. Crash against front door. Martha's laughter heard. Front door opens, lights are switched on. Martha enters, followed by George.

MARTHA. Jesus . . .

GEORGE. . . . Shhhhhhh . . .

MARTHA. . . . H. Christ . . .

GEORGE. For God's sake, Martha, it's two o'clock in the . . .

MARTHA. Oh, George!

GEORGE. Well, I'm sorry, but . . .

MARTHA. What a cluck! What a cluck you are.

GEORGE. It's late, you know? Late.

MARTHA. (*Looks about the room. Imitates Bette Davis.*) What a dump. Hey, what's that from? "What a dump!"

GEORGE. How would I know what . . .

MARTHA. Aw, come on! What's it from? *You* know. . . .

GEORGE. . . . Martha . . .

MARTHA. WHAT'S IT FROM, FOR CHRIST'S SAKE?

GEORGE. (*Wearily.*) What's what from?

MARTHA. I just told you; I just did it. "What a dump!" Hunh? What's that from?

GEORGE. I haven't the faintest idea what. . . .

MARTHA. Dumbbell! It's from some goddamn Bette Davis picture . . . some goddamn Warner Brothers epic. . . .

GEORGE. I can't remember all the pictures that . . .

MARTHA. Nobody's asking you to remember every single goddamn Warner Brothers epic . . . just one! One single little epic! Bette Davis gets peritonitis in the end . . . she's got this big

5

black fright wig she wears all through the picture and she gets peritonitis, and she's married to Joseph Cotten or something. . . .

GEORGE. . . . Some*body* . . .

MARTHA. . . . some*body* . . . and she wants to go to Chicago all the time, 'cause she's in love with that actor with the scar. . . . But she gets sick, and she sits down in front of her dressing table. . . .

GEORGE. What actor? What scar?

MARTHA. *I* can't remember his name, for God's sake. What's the name of the *picture*? I want to know what the name of the *picture* is. She sits down in front of her dressing table . . . and she's got this peritonitis . . . and she tries to put her lipstick on, but she can't . . . and she gets it all over her face . . . but she decides to go to Chicago anyway, and . . .

GEORGE. *Chicago!* It's called *Chicago.*

MARTHA. Hunh? What . . . what is?

GEORGE. The picture . . . it's called *Chicago.* . . .

MARTHA. Good grief! Don't you know *anything*? *Chicago* was a 'thirties musical, starring little Miss Alice *Faye.* Don't you know *anything*?

GEORGE. Well, that was probably before my *time,* but . . .

MARTHA. Can it! Just cut that out! This picture . . . Bette Davis comes home from a hard day at the grocery store. . . .

GEORGE. She works in a grocery store?

MARTHA. She's a housewife; she buys things . . . and she comes home with the groceries, and she walks into the modest living room of the modest cottage modest Joseph Cotten has set her up in. . . .

GEORGE. Are they married?

MARTHA. (*Impatiently.*) Yes. They're married. To each other. Cluck! And she comes in, and she looks around, and she puts her groceries down, and she says, "What a dump!"

GEORGE. (*Pause.*) Oh.

MARTHA. (*Pause.*) She's discontent.

GEORGE. (*Pause.*) Oh.

MARTHA. (*Pause.*) Well, what's the name of the picture?

GEORGE. I really don't know, Martha. . . .

MARTHA. Well, think!

GEORGE. I'm tired, dear . . . it's late . . . and besides . . .

MARTHA. I don't know what you're so tired about . . . you

haven't *done* anything all day; you didn't have any classes, or anything. . . .

GEORGE. Well, I'm tired. . . . If your father didn't set up these goddamn Saturday night orgies all the time . . .

MARTHA. Well, that's too bad about you, George. . . .

GEORGE. (*Grumbling.*) Well, that's how it is, anyway.

MARTHA. You didn't *do* anything; you never *do* anything; you never *mix*. You just sit around and *talk*.

GEORGE. What do you want me to do? Do you want me to act like you? Do you want me to go around all night *braying* at everybody, the way you do?

MARTHA. (*Braying.*) I DON'T BRAY!

GEORGE. (*Softly.*) All right . . . you don't bray.

MARTHA. (*Hurt.*) I do not *bray*.

GEORGE. All right. I said you didn't bray.

MARTHA. (*Pouting.*) Make me a drink.

GEORGE. What?

MARTHA. (*Still softly.*) I said, make me a drink.

GEORGE. (*Moving to the portable bar.*) Well, I don't suppose a nightcap'd kill either one of us. . . .

MARTHA. A nightcap! Are you kidding? We've got guests.

GEORGE. (*Disbelieving.*) We've got what?

MARTHA. Guests. GUESTS.

GEORGE. GUESTS!

MARTHA. Yes . . . guests . . . people. . . . We've got guests coming over.

GEORGE. When?

MARTHA. NOW!

GEORGE. Good Lord, Martha . . . do you know what time it . . . *Who's* coming over?

MARTHA. What's-their-name.

GEORGE. Who?

MARTHA. WHAT'S-THEIR-NAME!

GEORGE. Who what's-their name?

MARTHA. I don't know what their name is, George. . . . You met them tonight . . . they're new . . . he's in the math department, or something. . . .

GEORGE. Who . . . who are these people?

MARTHA. You met them tonight, George.

GEORGE. I don't remember meeting anyone tonight. . . .

7

MARTHA. Well you did. . . . Will you give me my drink, please. . . . He's in the math department . . . about thirty, blond, and . . .

GEORGE. . . . and good-looking. . . .

MARTHA. Yes . . . and good-looking. . . .

GEORGE. It figures.

MARTHA. . . . and his wife's a mousey little type, without any hips, or anything.

GEORGE. (*Vaguely.*) Oh.

MARTHA. You remember them now?

GEORGE. Yes, I guess so, Martha. . . . But why in God's name are they coming over here now?

MARTHA. (*In a so-there voice.*) Because Daddy said we should be nice to them, that's why.

GEORGE. (*Defeated.*) Oh, Lord.

MARTHA. May I have my drink, please? Daddy said we should be nice to them. Thank you.

GEORGE. But why now? It's after two o'clock in the morning, and . . .

MARTHA. Because Daddy said we should be nice to them!

GEORGE. Yes. But I'm sure your father didn't mean we were supposed to stay up all *night* with these people. I mean, we could have them over some Sunday or something. . . .

MARTHA. Well, never mind. . . . Besides, it *is* Sunday. Very early Sunday.

GEORGE. I mean . . . it's ridiculous. . . .

MARTHA. Well, it's *done!*

GEORGE. (*Resigned and exasperated.*) All right. Well . . . where are they? If we've got guests, where are they?

MARTHA. They'll be here soon.

GEORGE. What did they do . . . go home and get some sleep first, or something?

MARTHA. They'll *be* here!

GEORGE. I wish you'd *tell* me about something sometime. . . . I wish you'd stop *springing* things on me all the time.

MARTHA. I don't *spring* things on you all the time.

GEORGE. Yes, you do . . . you really do . . . you're always *springing* things on me.

MARTHA. (*Friendly-patronizing.*) Oh, George!

GEORGE. Always.

8

MARTHA. Poor Georgie-Porgie, put-upon pie! (*As he sulks.*) Awwwww . . . what are you doing? Are you sulking? Hunh? Let me see . . . are you sulking? Is that what you're doing?

GEORGE. (*Very quietly.*) Never mind, Martha. . . .

MARTHA. Awwwwwwwwww!

GEORGE. Just don't bother yourself. . . .

MARTHA. Awwwwwwwwww! (*No reaction.*) Hey! (*No reaction.*) HEY! (*George looks at her, put-upon.*) Hey. (*She sings.*)

> Who's afraid of Virginia Woolf,
> Virginia Woolf,
> Virginia Woolf. . . .

Ha, ha, ha, HA! (*No reaction.*) What's the matter . . . didn't you think that was funny? Hunh? (*Defiantly.*) I thought it was a scream . . . a real scream. You didn't like it, hunh?

GEORGE. It was all right, Martha. . . .

MARTHA. You laughed your head off when you heard it at the party.

GEORGE. I smiled. I didn't laugh my head off . . . I smiled, you know? . . . it was all right.

MARTHA. (*Gazing into her drink.*) You laughed your goddamn head off.

GEORGE. It was all right. . . .

MARTHA. (*Ugly.*) It was a scream!

GEORGE. (*Patiently.*) It was very funny, yes.

MARTHA. (*After a moment's consideration.*) You make me puke!

GEORGE. What?

MARTHA. Uh . . . you make me puke!

GEORGE. (*Thinks about it . . . then . . .*) That wasn't a very nice thing to say, Martha.

MARTHA. That wasn't *what*?

GEORGE. . . . a very nice thing to say.

MARTHA. I like your anger. I think that's what I like about you most . . . your anger. You're such a . . . such a simp! You don't even have the . . . the what? . . .

GEORGE. . . . guts? . . .

MARTHA. PHRASEMAKER! (*Pause . . . then they both laugh.*) Hey, put some more ice in my drink, will you? You never put any ice in my drink. Why is that, hunh?

GEORGE. (*Takes her drink.*) I always put ice in your drink. You

9

eat it, that's all. It's that habit you have . . . chewing your ice cubes . . . like a cocker spaniel. You'll crack your big teeth.

MARTHA. THEY'RE MY BIG TEETH!

GEORGE. Some of them . . . some of them.

MARTHA. I've got more teeth than you've got.

GEORGE. Two more.

MARTHA. Well, two more's a lot more.

GEORGE. I suppose it is. I suppose it's pretty remarkable . . . considering how old you are.

MARTHA. YOU CUT THAT OUT! (*Pause.*) You're not so young yourself.

GEORGE. (*With boyish pleasure . . . a chant.*) I'm six years younger than you are. . . . I always have been and I always will be.

MARTHA. (*Glumly.*) Well . . . you're going bald.

GEORGE. So are you. (*Pause . . . they both laugh.*) Hello, honey.

MARTHA. Hello. C'mon over here and give your Mommy a big sloppy kiss.

GEORGE. . . . oh, now . . .

MARTHA. I WANT A BIG SLOPPY KISS!

GEORGE. (*Preoccupied.*) I don't *want* to kiss you, Martha. Where *are* these people? Where are these *people* you invited over?

MARTHA. They stayed on to talk to Daddy. . . . They'll be here. . . . *Why* don't you want to kiss me?

GEORGE. (*Too matter-of-fact.*) Well, dear, if I kissed you I'd get all excited . . . I'd get beside myself, and I'd take you, by force, right here on the living room rug, and then our little guests would walk in, and . . . well, just think what your father would say about *that.*

MARTHA. You pig!

GEORGE. (*Haughtily.*) Oink! Oink!

MARTHA. Ha, ha, ha, HA! Make me another drink . . . lover.

GEORGE. (*Taking her glass.*) My God, you can swill it down, can't you?

MARTHA. (*Imitating a tiny child.*) I'm firsty.

GEORGE. Jesus!

MARTHA. (*Swinging around.*) Look, sweetheart, I can drink you under any goddamn table you want . . . so don't worry about me!

GEORGE. Martha, I gave you the prize years ago. . . . There isn't an abomination award going that you . . .

MARTHA. I swear . . . if you existed I'd divorce you. . . .

GEORGE. Well, just stay on your feet, that's all. . . . These people are your guests, you know, and . . .

MARTHA. I can't even see you . . . I haven't been able to see you for years. . . .

GEORGE. . . . if you pass out, or throw up, or something. . . .

MARTHA. . . . I mean, you're a blank, a cipher. . . .

GEORGE. . . . and try to keep your clothes on, too. There aren't many more sickening sights than you with a couple of drinks in you and your skirt up over your head, you know. . . .

MARTHA. . . . a zero. . . .

GEORGE. . . . your *heads*. I should say . . . (*The front door bell chimes.*)

MARTHA. Party! Party!

GEORGE. (*Murderously.*) I'm really looking forward to this, Martha. . . .

MARTHA. (*Same.*) Go answer the door.

GEORGE. (*Not moving.*) You answer it.

MARTHA. Get to that door, you. (*He does not move.*) I'll fix you, you . . .

GEORGE. (*Fake-spits.*) . . . to you . . . (*Door chime again.*)

MARTHA. (*Shouting . . . to the door.*) C'MON IN! (*To George, between her teeth.*) I said, get over there!

GEORGE. (*Moves a little toward the door, smiling slightly.*) All right, love . . . whatever love wants. (*Stops.*) Just don't start on the bit, that's all.

MARTHA. The bit? The bit? What kind of language is that? What are you talking about?

GEORGE. The bit. Just don't start in on the bit.

MARTHA. You imitating one of your students, for God's sake? What are you trying to do? WHAT BIT?

GEORGE. Just don't start in on the bit about the kid, that's all.

MARTHA. What do you take me for?

GEORGE. Much too much.

MARTHA. (*Really angered.*) Yeah? Well, I'll start in on the kid if I want to.

11

GEORGE. Just leave the kid out of this.

MARTHA. (*Threatening.*) He's mine as much as he is yours. I'll talk about him if I want to.

GEORGE. I'd advise against it, Martha.

MARTHA. Well, good for you. (*Knock.*) C'mon in. Get over there and open the door!

GEORGE. You've been advised.

MARTHA. Yeah . . . sure. Get over there!

GEORGE. (*Moving toward the door.*) All right, love . . . whatever love wants. Isn't it nice the way some people have manners, though, even in this day and age? Isn't it nice that some people won't just come breaking into other people's houses even if they *do* hear some sub-human monster yowling at 'em from inside . . . ?

MARTHA. SCREW YOU! (*Simultaneously with Martha's last remark, George flings open the front door. Honey and Nick are framed in the entrance. There is a brief silence, then . . .*)

GEORGE. (*Ostensibly a pleased recognition of Honey and Nick, but really satisfaction at having Martha's explosion overheard.*) Ahhhhhhhhh!

MARTHA. (*A little too loud . . . to cover.*) HI! Hi, there . . . c'mon in!

HONEY and NICK. (*Ad lib.*) Hello, here we are . . . hi . . . etc.

GEORGE. (*Very matter-of-factly.*) You must be our little guests.

MARTHA. Ha, ha, ha, HA! Just ignore old sour-puss over there. C'mon in, kids . . . give your coats and stuff to sour-puss.

NICK. (*Without expression.*) Well, now, perhaps we shouldn't have come. . . .

HONEY. Yes . . . it *is* late, and . . .

MARTHA. Late! Are you kidding? Throw your stuff down anywhere and c'mon in.

GEORGE. (*Vaguely . . . walking away.*) Anywhere . . . furniture, floor . . . doesn't make any difference around this place.

NICK. (*To Honey.*) I told you we shouldn't have come.

MARTHA. (*Stentorian.*) I said c'mon in! Now c'mon!

HONEY. (*Giggling a little as she and Nick advance.*) Oh, dear.

GEORGE. (*Imitating Honey's giggle.*) Hee, hee, hee, hee.

MARTHA. *Swinging on George.*) Look, muckmouth . . . you cut that out!

GEORGE. (*Innocence and hurt.*) Martha! (*To Honey and Nick.*) Martha's a devil with language; she really is.

MARTHA. Hey, *kids* . . . sit down.

HONEY. (*As she sits.*) Oh, isn't this lovely!

NICK. (*Perfunctorily.*) Yes indeed . . . very handsome.

MARTHA. Well, thanks.

NICK. (*Indicating the abstract painting.*) Who . . . who did the . . . ?

MARTHA. That? Oh; that's by . . .

GEORGE. . . . some Greek with a mustache Martha attacked one night in . . .

HONEY. (*To save the situation.*) Oh, ho, ho, ho, HO.

NICK. It's got a . . . a . . .

GEORGE. A quiet intensity?

NICK. Well, no . . . a . . .

GEORGE. Oh. (*Pause.*) Well, then, a certain noisy relaxed quality, maybe?

NICK. (*Knows what George is doing, but stays grimly, coolly polite.*) No. What I meant was . . .

GEORGE. How about . . . uh . . . a quietly noisy relaxed intensity.

HONEY. Dear! You're being joshed.

NICK. (*Cold.*) I'm aware of that. (*A brief, awkward silence.*)

GEORGE. (*Truly.*) I *am* sorry. (*Nick nods condescending forgiveness.*) What it is, actually, is it's a pictorial representation of the order of Martha's mind.

MARTHA. Ha, ha, ha, HA! Make the kids a drink, George. What do you want, kids? What do you want to drink, hunh?

NICK. Honey? What would you like?

HONEY. I don't know, dear . . . A little brandy, maybe. "Never mix—never worry." (*She giggles.*)

GEORGE. Brandy? Just brandy? Simple; simple. (*Moves to the portable bar.*) What about you . . . uh. . . .

NICK. Bourbon on the rocks, if you don't mind.

GEORGE. (*As he makes drinks.*) Mind? No, I don't mind. I don't think I mind. Martha? Rubbing alcohol for you?

MARTHA. Sure. "Never mix—never worry."

GEORGE. Martha's tastes in liquor have come down . . . simplified over the years . . . crystallized. Back when I was courting

13

Martha—well, I don't know if that's exactly the right word for it—but back when I was courting Martha . . .

MARTHA. (*Cheerfully.*) Screw, sweetie!

GEORGE. (*Returning with Honey and Nick's drinks.*) At any rate, back when I was courting Martha, she'd order the damnedest things! You wouldn't believe it! We'd go into a bar . . . you know, a *bar* . . . a whiskey, beer, and bourbon *bar* . . . and what she'd do would be, she'd screw up her face, think real hard, come up with . . . brandy Alexanders, creme de cacao frappes, gimlets, flaming punch bowls . . . seven layer liqueur things.

MARTHA. They were good . . . I liked them.

GEORGE. Real lady-like little drinkies.

MARTHA. Hey, where's my rubbing alcohol?

GEORGE. (*Returning to the portable bar.*) But the years have brought to Martha a sense of essentials . . . the knowledge that cream is for coffee, lime juice for pies . . . and alcohol (*Brings Martha her drink.*) pure and simple . . . here you are, angel . . . for the pure and simple. (*Raises his glass.*) For the mind's blind eye, the heart's ease, and the liver's craw. Down the hatch, all.

MARTHA. (*To them all.*) Cheers, dears. (*They all drink.*) You have a poetic nature, George . . . a Dylan Thomas-y quality that gets me right where I live.

GEORGE. Vulgar girl! With guests here!

MARTHA. Ha, ha, ha, HA! (*To Honey and Nick.*) Hey; hey! (*Sings, conducts with her drink in her hand. Honey joins in toward the end.*)

> Who's afraid of Virginia Woolf,
> Virginia Woolf,
> Virginia Woolf,
> Who's afraid of Virginia Woolf. . . .

(*Martha and Honey laugh; Nick smiles.*)

HONEY. Oh, wasn't that funny? That was so funny. . . .

NICK. (*Snapping to.*) Yes . . . yes, it was.

MARTHA. I thought I'd bust a gut; I really did. . . . I really thought I'd bust a gut laughing. George didn't like it. . . . George didn't think it was funny at all.

GEORGE. Lord, Martha, do we have to go through this again?

MARTHA. I'm trying to shame you into a sense of humor, angel, that's all.

GEORGE. (*Over-patiently, to Honey and Nick.*) Martha didn't think I laughed loud enough. Martha thinks that unless . . . as she demurely puts it . . . that unless you "bust a gut" you aren't amused. You know? Unless you carry on like a hyena you aren't having any fun.

HONEY. Well, I certainly had fun . . . it was a *wonderful* party.

NICK. (*Attempting enthusiasm.*) Yes . . . it certainly was.

HONEY. (*To Martha.*) And your father! Oh! He is so marvelous!

NICK. (*As above.*) Yes . . . yes, he is.

HONEY. Oh, I tell you.

MARTHA. (*Genuinely proud.*) He's quite a guy, isn't he? Quite a guy.

GEORGE. (*At Nick.*) And you'd better believe it!

HONEY. (*Admonishing George.*) Ohhhhhhhhh! He's a wonderful man.

GEORGE. I'm not trying to tear him down. He's a God, we all know that.

MARTHA. You lay off my father!

GEORGE. Yes, love. (*To Nick.*) All I mean is . . . when you've had as many of these faculty parties as I have . . .

NICK. (*Killing the attempted rapport.*) I rather appreciated it. I mean, aside from enjoying it, I appreciated it. You know, when you're new at a place. . . . (*George eyes him suspiciously.*) Meeting everyone, getting introduced around . . . getting to know some of the men. . . . When I was teaching in Kansas . . .

HONEY. You won't believe it, but we had to make our way all by *ourselves* . . . isn't that right, dear?

NICK. Yes, it is. . . . We . . .

HONEY. . . . We had to make our own way. . . . I had to go up to wives . . . in the library, or at the supermarket . . . and say, "Hello, I'm new here . . . you must be Mrs. So-and-so, Doctor So-and-so's wife." It really wasn't very nice at all.

MARTHA. Well, *Daddy* knows how to run things.

NICK. (*Not enough enthusiasm.*) He's a remarkable man.

MARTHA. You bet your sweet life.

GEORGE. (*To Nick . . . a confidence, but not whispered.*) Let me tell you a secret, baby. There are easier things in the world,

15

if you happen to be teaching at a university, there are easier things than being married to the daughter of the president of that university. There are easier things in this world.

MARTHA. (*Loud . . . to no one in particular.*) It *should* be an extraordinary opportunity . . . for *some* men it would be the chance of a lifetime!

GEORGE. (*To Nick . . . a solemn wink.*) There are, believe me, easier things in this world.

NICK. Well, I can understand how it might make for some . . . awkwardness, perhaps . . . conceivably, but . . .

MARTHA. *Some* men would give their right arm for the chance!

GEORGE. (*Quietly.*) Alas, Martha, in reality it works out that the sacrifice is usually of a somewhat more private portion of the anatomy.

MARTHA. (*A snarl of dismissal and contempt.*) NYYYY-AAAAHHHHH!

HONEY. (*Rising quickly.*) I wonder if you could show me where the . . . (*Her voice trails off.*)

GEORGE. (*To Martha, indicating Honey.*) Martha. . . .

NICK. (*To Honey.*) Are you all right?

HONEY. Of course, dear. I want to . . . put some powder on my nose.

GEORGE. (*As Martha is not getting up.*) Martha, won't you show her where we keep the . . . euphemism?

MARTHA. Hm? What? Oh! Sure! (*Rises.*) I'm sorry, c'mon. I want to show you the house.

HONEY. I think I'd like to . . .

MARTHA. . . . wash up? Sure . . . c'mon with me. (*Takes Honey by the arm. To the men.*) You two do some men talk for a while.

HONEY. (*To Nick.*) We'll be back, dear.

MARTHA. (*To George.*) Honestly, George, you burn me up!

GEORGE. (*Happily.*) All right.

MARTHA. You really do, George.

GEORGE. O.K. Martha . . . O.K. Just . . . trot along.

MARTHA. You really do.

GEORGE Just don't shoot your mouth off . . . about . . . you-know what.

MARTHA. (*Surprisingly vehement.*) I'll talk about any goddamn thing I want to, George!

GEORGE. O.K. O.K. Vanish.

MARTHA. Any goddamn thing I want to! (*Practically dragging Honey out with her.*) C'mon. . . .

GEORGE. Vanish. (*The women have gone.*) So? What'll it be?

NICK. Oh, I don't know . . . I'll stick to bourbon, I guess.

GEORGE. (*Takes Nick's glass, goes to portable bar.*) That what you were drinking over at Parnassus?

NICK. Over at . . . ?

GEORGE. Parnassus.

NICK. I don't understand. . . .

GEORGE. Skip it. (*Hands him his drink.*) One bourbon.

NICK. Thanks.

GEORGE. It's just a private joke between li'l ol' Martha and me. (*They sit.*) So? (*Pause.*) So . . . you're in the math department, eh?

NICK. No . . . uh, no.

GEORGE. Martha said you were. I think that's what she said. (*Not too friendly.*) What made you decide to be a teacher?

NICK. Oh . . . well, the same things that . . . uh . . . motivated you, I imagine.

GEORGE. What were they?

NICK. (*Formal.*) Pardon?

GEORGE. I said, what were they? What were the things that motivated me?

NICK. (*Laughing uneasily.*) Well . . . I'm sure I don't know.

GEORGE. You just finished saying that the things that motivated you were the same things that motivated me.

NICK. (*With a little pique.*) I said I *imagined* they were.

GEORGE. Oh. (*Off-hand.*) Did you? (*Pause.*) Well. . . . (*Pause.*) You like it here?

NICK. (*Looking about the room.*) Yes . . . it's . . . it's fine.

GEORGE. I mean the University.

NICK. Oh. . . . I thought you meant . . .

GEORGE. Yes . . . I can see you did. (*Pause.*) I meant the University.

NICK. Well, I . . . I like it . . . fine. (*As George just stares at him.*) Just fine. (*Same.*) You . . . you've been here quite a long time, haven't you?

GEORGE. (*Absently, as if he had not heard.*) What? Oh . . . yes. Ever since I married . . . uh, what's-her-name . . . uh,

17

Martha. Even before that. (*Pause.*) Forever. (*To himself.*) Dashed hopes, and good intentions. Good, better, best, bested. (*Back to Nick.*) How do you like that for a declension, young man? Eh?

NICK. Sir, I'm sorry if we . . .

GEORGE. (*With an edge in his voice.*) You didn't answer my question.

NICK. Sir?

GEORGE. Don't you condescend to me! (*Toying with him.*) I asked you how you liked that for a declension: Good; better; best; bested. Hm? Well?

NICK. (*With some distaste.*) I really don't know what to say.

GEORGE. (*Feigned incredulousness.*) You really don't know what to *say?*

NICK. (*Snapping it out.*) All right . . . what do you want me to say? Do you want me to say it's funny, so you can contradict me and say it's sad? or do you want me to say it's sad so you can turn around and say no, it's funny. You can play that damn little game any way you want to, you know!

GEORGE. (*Feigned awe.*) Very good! Very good!

NICK. (*Even angrier than before.*) And when my wife comes back, I think we'll just . . .

GEORGE. (*Sincere.*) Now, now . . . calm down, my boy. Just . . . calm . . . down. (*Pause.*) All right? (*Pause.*) You want another drink? Here, give me your glass.

NICK. I still have one. I *do* think that when my wife comes downstairs . . .

GEORGE. Here . . . I'll freshen it. Give me your glass. (*Takes it.*)

NICK. What I mean is . . . you two . . . you and your wife . . . seem to be having *some* sort of a . . .

GEORGE. Martha and I are having . . . nothing. Martha and I are merely . . . exercising . . . that's all . . . we're merely walking what's left of our wits. Don't pay any attention to it.

NICK. (*Undecided.*) Still . . .

GEORGE. (*An abrupt change of pace.*) Well, now . . . let's sit down and talk, hunh?

NICK. (*Cool again.*) It's just that I don't like to . . . become involved . . . (*An afterthought.*) uh . . . in other people's affairs.

GEORGE. (*Comforting a child.*) Well, you'll get over that . . .

18

small college and all. Musical beds is the faculty sport around here.

NICK. Sir?

GEORGE. I said, musical beds is the faculty. . . . Never mind. I wish you wouldn't go "Sir" like that . . . not with the question mark at the end of it. You know? Sir? I know it's meant to be a sign of respect for your (*Winces.*) elders . . . but . . . uh . . . the way you do it. . . . Uh . . . Sir? . . . Madam?

NICK. (*With a small, noncommittal smile*) No disrespect intended.

GEORGE. How old *are* you?

NICK. Twenty-eight.

GEORGE. I'm forty something. (*Waits for reaction . . . gets none.*) Aren't you surprised? I mean . . . don't I look older? Doesn't this . . . *gray* quality suggest the fifties? Don't I sort of fade into backgrounds . . . get lost in the cigarette smoke? Hunh?

NICK. (*Looking around for an ash tray.*) I think you look . . . fine.

GEORGE. I've always been lean . . . I haven't put on five pounds since I was your age. I don't have a paunch, either. . . . What I've got . . . I've got this little distension just below the belt . . . but it's hard . . . It's not soft flesh. I use the handball courts. How much do *you* weigh?

NICK. I . . .

GEORGE. Hundred and fifty-five, sixty . . . something like that? Do you play handball?

NICK. Well, yes . . . no . . . I mean, not very well.

GEORGE. Well, then . . . we shall play some time. Martha is a hundred and eight . . . years old. She weighs somewhat more than that. How old is *your* wife?

NICK. (*A little bewildered.*) She's twenty-six.

GEORGE. Martha is a remarkable woman. I would imagine she weighs around a hundred and ten.

NICK. Your . . . wife . . . weighs . . . ?

GEORGE. No, no, my boy. Yours! *Your* wife. My wife is Martha.

NICK. Yes . . . I know.

GEORGE. If you were married to Martha you would know what it means. (*Pause.*) But then, if I were married to your wife I would know what that means, too . . . wouldn't I?

19

NICK. (*After a pause.*) Yes.

GEORGE. Martha says you're in the Math Department, or something.

NICK. (*As if for the hundredth time.*) No . . . I'm not.

GEORGE. Martha is seldom mistaken . . . maybe you *should* be in the Math Department, or something.

NICK. I'm a biologist. I'm in the Biology Department.

GEORGE. (*After a pause.*) Oh. (*Then, as if remembering something.*) OH!

NICK. Sir?

GEORGE. You're the one! You're the one's going to make all that trouble . . . making everyone the same, rearranging the chromozones, or whatever it is. Isn't that right?

NICK. (*With that small smile.*) Not exactly: chromosomes.

GEORGE. I'm very mistrustful. Do you believe . . . (*Shifting in his chair.*) . . . do you believe that people learn nothing from history? Not that there is nothing to learn, mind you, but that people learn nothing? I am in the History Department.

NICK. Well . . .

GEORGE. I am a Doctor. A.B. . . . M.A. . . . PH.D. . . . AB-MAPHID! Abmaphid has been variously described as a wasting disease of the frontal lobes, and as a wonder drug. It is actually both. I'm really very mistrustful. Biology, hunh? (*Nick does not answer . . . nods . . . looks.*) I read somewhere that science fiction is really not fiction at all . . . that you people are rearranging my genes, so that everyone will be like everyone else. Now, I won't have that! It would be a . . . shame. I mean . . . look at me! Is it really such a good idea . . . if everyone was forty something and looked fifty-five? You didn't answer my question about history.

NICK. This genetic business you're talking about. . . .

GEORGE. Oh, that. (*Dismisses it with a wave of his hand.*) That's very upsetting . . . very . . . disappointing. But history is a great deal more . . . disappointing. I am in the History Department.

NICK. Yes . . . you told me.

GEORGE. I know I told you. . . . I shall probably tell you several more times. Martha tells me often, that I am *in* the History Department . . . as opposed to *being* the History Department

. . . in the sense of *running* the History Department. I do not run the History Department.

NICK. Well, I don't run the Biology Department.

GEORGE. You're twenty-one!

NICK. Twenty-eight.

GEORGE. Twenty-eight! Perhaps when you're forty something and look fifty-five, you will run the History Department. . . .

NICK. . . . Biology . . .

GEORGE. . . . the Biology Department. I *did* run the History Department, for four years, during the war, but that was because everybody was away. Then . . . everybody came back . . . because nobody got killed. That's New England for you. Isn't that amazing? Not one single man in this whole place got his head shot off. That's pretty irrational. (*Broods.*) Your wife *doesn't* have any hips . . . has she . . . does she?

NICK. What?

GEORGE. I don't mean to suggest that I'm hip-happy. . . . I'm not one of those thirty-six, twenty-two, seventy-eight men. No-siree . . . not me. Everything in proportion. I was implying that your wife is . . . slim-hipped.

NICK. Yes . . . she is.

GEORGE. (*Looking at the ceiling.*) What are they *doing* up there? I assume that's where they are.

NICK. (*False heartiness.*) You know women.

GEORGE. (*Gives Nick a long stare, of feigned incredulity . . . then his attention moves.*) Not one son-of-a-bitch got killed. Of course, nobody bombed Washington. No . . . that's not fair. You have any kids?

NICK. Uh . . . no . . . not yet. (*Pause.*) You?

GEORGE. (*A kind of challenge.*) That's for me to know and you to find out.

NICK. Indeed?

GEORGE. No kids, hunh?

NICK. Not yet.

GEORGE. People do . . . uh . . . have kids. That's what I meant about history. You people are going to make them in test tubes, aren't you? You biologists. Babies. Then the rest of us . . . them as wants to . . . can screw to their heart's content. What will happen to the tax deduction? Has anyone figured that out yet? (*Nick, who can think of nothing better to do, laughs mildly.*) But you *are* going to have kids . . . anyway. In spite of history.

NICK. (*Hedging.*) *Yes* . . . certainly. We . . . want to wait . . . a little . . . until we're settled.

GEORGE. And this . . . (*With a handsweep taking in not only the room, the house, but the whole countryside.*) . . . this is your heart's content—Illyria . . . Penguin Island . . . Gomorrah. . . . You think you're going to be happy here in New Carthage, eh?

NICK. (*A little defensively.*) I hope we'll stay here.

GEORGE. And every definition has its boundaries, eh? Well, it isn't a bad college, I guess. I mean . . . it'll do. It isn't M.I.T. . . . it isn't U.C.L.A. . . . it isn't the Sorbonne . . . or Moscow U. either, for that matter.

NICK. I don't mean . . . forever.

GEORGE. Well, don't you let that get bandied about. The old man wouldn't like it. Martha's father expects loyalty and devotion out of his . . . staff. I was going to use another word. Martha's father expects his . . . staff . . . to cling to the walls of this place, like the ivy . . . to come here and grow old . . . to fall in the line of service. One man, a professor of Latin and Elocution, actually fell in the cafeteria line, one lunch. He was buried, as many of us have been, and as many more of us will be, under the shrubbery around the chapel. It is said . . . and I have no reason to doubt it . . . that we make excellent fertilizer. But the old man is not going to be buried under the shrubbery . . . the old man is not going to die. Martha's father has the staying power of one of those Micronesian tortoises. There are rumors . . . which you must not breathe in front of Martha, for she foams at the mouth . . . that the old man, her father, is over two hundred years old. There is probably an irony involved in this, but I am not drunk enough to figure out what it is. How many kids you going to have?

NICK. I . . . I don't know. . . . My wife is . . .

GEORGE. Slim-hipped. (*Rises.*) Have a drink.

NICK. Yes.

GEORGE. MARTHA! (*No answer.*) DAMN IT! (*To Nick.*) You asked me if I knew women. . . . Well, one of the things I do *not* know about them is what they talk about while the men are talking. (*Vaguely.*) I must find out some time.

22

MARTHA'S VOICE. WHADD'YA WANT?

GEORGE. (*To Nick.*) Isn't that a wonderful sound? What I mean is . . . what do you think they really *talk* about . . . or don't you care?

NICK. Themselves, I would imagine.

MARTHA'S VOICE. GEORGE?

GEORGE. (*To Nick.*) Do you find women . . . puzzling?

NICK. Well . . . yes and no.

GEORGE. (*With a knowing nod.*) Unh-hunh. (*Moves toward the hall, almost bumps into Honey, re-entering.*) Oh! Well, here's one of you, at least. (*Honey moves toward Nick. George goes to the hall.*)

HONEY. (*To George.*) She'll be right down. (*To Nick.*) You must see this house, dear . . . this is such a wonderful old house.

NICK. Yes, I . . .

GEORGE. MARTHA!

MARTHA'S VOICE. FOR CHRIST'S SAKE, HANG ON A MINUTE, WILL YOU?

HONEY. (*To George.*) She'll be right down . . . she's changing.

GEORGE. (*Incredulous.*) She's *what?* She's changing?

HONEY. Yes.

GEORGE. Her clothes?

HONEY. Her dress.

GEORGE. (*Suspicious.*) Why?

HONEY. (*With a nervous little laugh.*) Why, I imagine she wants to be . . . comfortable.

GEORGE. (*With a threatening look toward the hall.*) Oh she does, does she?

HONEY. Well, heavens, I should think . . .

GEORGE. YOU DON'T KNOW!

NICK. (*As Honey starts.*) You feel all right?

HONEY. (*Reassuring, but with the echo of a whine. A long-practiced tone.*) Oh, yes, dear . . . perfectly fine.

GEORGE. (*Fuming . . . to himself.*) So she wants to be comfortable, does she? Well, we'll see about that.

HONEY. (*To George, brightly.*) I didn't know until just a minute ago than you had a *son*.

GEORGE. (*Wheeling, as if struck from behind.*) WHAT?

HONEY. A son! I hadn't known.

23

NICK. You to know and me to find out. Well, he must be quite a big . . .

HONEY. Twenty-one . . . twenty-one tomorrow . . . tomorrow's his birthday.

NICK. (*A victorious smile.*) Well!

GEORGE. (*To Honey.*) She told you about him?

HONEY. (*Flustered.*) Well, yes. Well, I mean . . .

GEORGE. (*Nailing it down.*) She told you about him.

HONEY. (*A nervous giggle.*) Yes.

GEORGE. (*Strangely.*) You say she's changing?

HONEY. Yes. . . .

GEORGE. And she mentioned . . . ?

HONEY. (*Cheerful, but a little puzzled.*) . . . your son's birthday . . . yes.

GEORGE. (*More or less to himself.*) O.K., Martha . . . O.K.

NICK. You look pale, Honey. Do you want a . . ¸ ?

HONEY. Yes, dear . . . a little more brandy, maybe. Just a drop.

GEORGE. O.K., Martha.

NICK. May I use the . . . uh . . . bar?

GEORGE. Hm? Oh, yes . . . yes . . . by all means. Drink away . . . you'll need it as the years go on. (*For Martha, as if she were in the room.*) You goddamn destructive . . .

HONEY. (*To cover.*) What time is it, dear?

NICK. Two-thirty.

HONEY. Oh, it's so late . . . we *should* be getting home.

GEORGE. (*Nastily, but he is so preoccupied he hardly notices his own tone.*) For what? You keeping the babysitter up, or something?

NICK. (*Almost a warning.*) I told you we didn't have children.

GEORGE. Hm? (*Realizing.*) Oh, I'm sorry. I wasn't even listening . . . or thinking . . . (*With a flick of his hand.*) . . . whichever one applies.

NICK. (*Softly, to Honey.*) We'll go in a little while.

GEORGE. (*Driving.*) Oh, no, now . . . you mustn't. Martha is changing . . . and Martha is not changing for me. Martha hasn't changed for *me* in years. If Martha is changing, it means we'll be here for . . . days. You are being accorded an honor, and you must not forget that Martha is the daughter of our beloved boss. She is his . . . right ball, you might say.

24

NICK. You might not understand this . . . but I wish you wouldn't talk that way in front of my wife.

HONEY. Oh, now . . .

GEORGE. (*Incredulous.*) Really? Well, you're quite right. We'll leave that sort of talk to Martha.

MARTHA. (*Entering.*) What sort of talk? (*Martha has changed her clothes, and she looks, now, more comfortable and . . . and this is most important . . . most voluptuous.*)

GEORGE. There you are, my pet.

NICK. (*Impressed, rising.*) Well, now . . .

GEORGE. Why, Martha . . . your Sunday chapel dress!

HONEY. (*Slightly disapproving.*) Oh, that's most attractive.

MARTHA. (*Showing off.*) You like it? Good! (*To George.*) What the hell do you mean screaming up the stairs at me like that?

GEORGE. We got lonely, darling . . . we got lonely for the soft purr of your little voice.

MARTHA. (*Deciding not to rise to it.*) Oh. Well, then, you just trot over to the barie-poo . . .

GEORGE. (*Taking the tone from her.*) . . . and make your little mommy a gweat big dwink.

MARTHA. (*Giggles.*) That's right. (*To Nick.*) Well, did you two have a nice little talk? You men solve the problems of the world, as usual?

NICK. Well, no, we . . .

GEORGE. (*Quickly.*) What we did, actually, if you really want to know, what we did actually is try to figure out what you two were talking about. (*Honey giggles, Martha laughs.*)

MARTHA. (*To Honey.*) Aren't they something? Aren't these . . . (*Cheerfully disdainful.*) . . . men the absolute end? (*To George.*) Why didn't you sneak upstairs and listen in?

GEORGE. Oh, I wouldn't have *listened,* Martha. . . . I would have peeked. (*Honey giggles, Martha laughs.*)

NICK. (*To George, with false heartiness.*) It's a conspiracy.

GEORGE. And now we'll never know. Shucks!

MARTHA. (*To Nick, as Honey beams.*) Hey, you must be quite a boy, getting your Masters when you were . . . what? . . . twelve? You hear that, George?

NICK. Twelve-and-a-half, actually. No, nineteen really. (*To Honey.*) Honey, you needn't have mentioned that. It . . .

HONEY. Ohhhh . . . I'm *proud* of you. . . .

GEORGE. (*Seriously, if sadly.*) That's very . . . impressive.

MARTHA. (*Aggressively.*) You're damned right!

GEORGE. (*Between his teeth.*) I said I was impressed, Martha. I'm beside myself with jealousy. What do you want me to do, throw up? (*To Nick.*) That really is very impressive. (*To Honey.*) You should be right proud.

HONEY. (*Coy.*) Oh, he's a pretty nice fella.

GEORGE. (*To Nick.*) I wouldn't be surprised if you *did* take over the History Department one of these days.

NICK. The Biology Department.

GEORGE. The *Biology* Department . . . of course. I seem preoccupied with history. Oh! What a remark. (*He strikes a pose, his hand over his heart, his head raised, his voice stentorian.*) "I am preoccupied with history."

MARTHA. (*As Honey and Nick chuckle.*) Ha, ha, ha, HA!

GEORGE. (*With some disgust.*) I think I'll make *myself* a drink.

MARTHA. George is not preoccupied with *history*. . . . George is preoccupied with the *History Department.* George is preoccupied with the History Department because . . .

GEORGE. . . . because he is *not* the History Department, but is only *in* the History Department. We know, Martha . . . we went all through it while you were upstairs . . . getting up. There's no need to go through it again.

MARTHA. That's right, baby . . . keep it clean. (*To the others.*) George is bogged down in the History Department. He's an old bog in the History Department, that's what George is. A bog. . . . A fen. . . . A G.D. swamp. Ha, ha, ha, HA! A SWAMP! Hey, swamp! Hey, SWAMPY!

GEORGE. (*With a great effort controls himself . . . then, as if she had said nothing more than "George, dear" . . .*) Yes, Martha? Can I get you something?

MARTHA. (*Amused at his game.*) Well . . . uh . . . sure, you can light my cigarette, if you're of a mind to.

GEORGE. (*Considers, then moves off.*) No . . . there are limits. I mean, man can put up with only so much without he descends a rung or two on the old evolutionary ladder . . . (*Now a quick aside to Nick.*) . . . which is up your line . . . (*Then back to Martha.*) . . . sinks, Martha, and it's a funny ladder . . . you can't reverse yourself . . . start back up once you're

26

descending. (*Martha blows him an arrogant kiss.*) Now . . . I'll hold your hand when it's dark and you're afraid of the bogey man, and I'll tote your gin bottles out after midnight, so no one'll see . . . but I will not light your cigarette. And that, as they say, is that. (*Brief silence.*)

MARTHA. (*Under her breath.*) Jesus! (*Then, immediately, to Nick.*) Hey, you played football, hunh?

HONEY. (*As Nick seems sunk in thought.*) Dear . . .

NICK. Oh! Oh, yes . . . I was a . . . quarterback . . . but I was much more . . . adept . . . at boxing, really.

MARTHA. (*With great enthusiasm.*) BOXING! You hear that, George?

GEORGE. (*Resignedly.*) Yes, Martha.

MARTHA. (*To Nick, with peculiar intensity and enthusiasm.*) You musta been pretty good at it . . . I mean, you don't look like you got hit in the face at all.

HONEY. (*Proudly.*) He was intercollegiate state middleweight champion.

NICK. (*Embarrassed.*) Honey . . .

HONEY. Well, you were.

MARTHA. You look like you still got a pretty good body *now*, too . . . is that right? Have you?

GEORGE. (*Intensely.*) Martha . . . decency forbids. . . .

MARTHA. (*To George . . . still staring at Nick, though.*) SHUT UP! (*Now, back to Nick.*) Well, have you? Have you kept your body?

NICK. (*Unselfconscious . . . almost encouraging her.*) It's still pretty good. I work out.

MARTHA. (*With a half-smile.*) Do you!

NICK. Yeah.

HONEY. Oh, yes . . . he has a very . . . firm body.

MARTHA. (*Still with that smile . . . a private communication with Nick.*) Have you! Oh, I think that's very nice.

NICK. (*Narcissistic, but not directly for Martha.*) Well, you never know . . . (*Shrugs.*) . . . you know . . . once you have it . . .

MARTHA. . . . you never know when it's going to come in handy.

NICK. I was going to say . . . why give it up until you have to.

MARTHA. I couldn't agree with you more. (*They both smile,*

27

and there is a rapport of some unformed sort, established.) I couldn't agree with you more.

GEORGE. Martha, your obscenity is more than . . .

MARTHA. George, here, doesn't cotton much to body talk . . . do you, sweetheart? (*No reply.*) George isn't too happy when we get to muscle. You know . . . flat bellies, pectorals . . .

GEORGE. (*To Honey.*) Would you like to take a walk around the garden?

HONEY. (*Chiding.*) Oh, now. . . .

GEORGE. (*Incredulous.*) You're amused? (*Shrugs.*) All right.

MARTHA. Paunchy over there isn't too happy when the conversation moves to muscle. How much do you weigh?

NICK. A hundred and fifty-five, a hundred and . . .

MARTHA. Still at the old middleweight limit, eh? That's pretty good. (*Swings around.*) Hey, George, tell 'em about the boxing match *we* had.

GEORGE. (*Slamming his drink down, moving toward the hall.*) Christ!

MARTHA. George! Tell 'em about it!

GEORGE. (*With a sick look on his face.*) You tell them, Martha. You're good at it. (*Exits.*)

HONEY. Is he . . . all right?

MARTHA. (*Laughs.*) Him? Oh, sure. George and I had this boxing match . . . Oh, Lord, twenty years ago . . . a couple of years after we were married.

NICK. A boxing match? The two of you?

HONEY. Really?

MARTHA. Yup . . . the two of us . . . really.

HONEY. (*With a little shivery giggle of anticipation.*) I can't imagine it.

MARTHA. Well, like I say, it was twenty years ago, and it wasn't in a ring, or anything like that, you know what I mean. It was wartime, and Daddy was on this physical fitness kick . . . Daddy's always admired physical fitness . . . says a man is only part brain . . . he has a body, too, and it's his responsibility to keep both of them up . . . you know?

NICK. Unh-hunh.

MARTHA. Says the brain can't work unless the body's working, too.

NICK. Well, that's not exactly so. . . .

MARTHA. Well, maybe that *isn't* what he says . . . something like it. *But* . . . it was wartime, and Daddy got the idea all the men should learn how to box . . . self-defense. I suppose the idea was if the Germans landed on the coast, or something, the whole faculty'd go out and punch 'em to death. . . . I don't know.

NICK. It was probably more the principle of the thing.

MARTHA. No kidding. Anyway, so Daddy had a couple of us over one Sunday and we went out in the back, and Daddy put on the gloves himself. Daddy's a strong man. . . . Well, *you* know.

NICK. Yes . . . yes.

MARTHA. And he asked George to box with him. Aaaaannnnd . . . George didn't *want* to . . . probably something about not wanting to bloody-up his meal ticket. . . .

NICK. Unh-hunh.

MARTHA. . . . Anyway, George said he didn't want to, and Daddy was saying, "Come on, young man . . . what sort of son-in-law *are* you?" . . . and stuff like that.

NICK. Yeah.

MARTHA. So, while this was going on . . . I don't know why I *did* it . . . I got into a pair of gloves myself . . . you know, I didn't lace 'em up, or anything . . . and I snuck up behind George, just kidding, and I yelled "Hey George!" and at the same time I let go sort of a roundhouse right . . . just kidding, you know?

NICK. Unh-hunh.

MARTHA. . . . and George wheeled around real quick, and he caught it right in the jaw . . . POW! (*Nick laughs.*) I hadn't meant it . . . honestly. Anyway . . . POW! Right in the jaw . . . and he was off balance . . . he must have been . . . and he stumbled back a few steps, and then, CRASH, he landed . . flat . . . in a huckleberry bush! (*Nick laughs. Honey goes tsk, tsk, tsk, tsk, and shakes her head.*) It was awful, really. It was funny, but it was awful. (*She thinks, gives a muffled laugh in rueful contemplation of the incident.*) I think it's colored our whole life. Really I do! It's an excuse, anyway. (*George enters now, his hands behind his back. No one sees him.*) It's what he uses for being bogged down, anyway . . . why he hasn't *gone* anywhere. (*George advances. Honey sees him.*) And it was an *accident* . . . a real, goddamn accident! (*George takes from behind his back a*

29

short-barreled shotgun, and calmly aims it at the back of Martha's head. Honey screams . . . rises. Nick rises, and, simultaneously, Martha turns her head to face George. George pulls the trigger.)

GEORGE. POW!!! *(Pop! From the barrel of the gun blossoms a large red and yellow Chinese parasol. Honey screams again, this time less, and mostly from relief and confusion.)* You're dead! Pow! You're dead!

NICK. *(Laughing.)* Good Lord. *(Honey is beside herself. Martha laughs too . . . almost breaks down, her great laugh booming. George joins in the general laughter and confusion. It dies, eventually.)*

HONEY. Oh! My goodness!

MARTHA. *(Joyously.)* Where'd you get that, you bastard?

NICK. *(His hand out for the gun.)* Let me see that, will you? *(George hands him the gun.)*

HONEY. I've never been so frightened in my life! Never!

GEORGE. *(A trifle abstracted.)* Oh, I've had it awhile. Did you like that?

MARTHA. *(Giggling.)* You bastard.

HONEY. *(Wanting attention.)* I've *never* been so frightened . . . never.

NICK. This is quite a gadget.

GEORGE. *(Leaning over Martha.)* You liked that, did you?

MARTHA. Yeah . . . that was pretty good. *(Softer.)* C'mon . . . give me a kiss.

GEORGE. *(Indicating Nick and Honey.)* Later, sweetie. *(But Martha will not be dissuaded. They kiss, George standing, leaning over Martha's chair. She takes his hand, places it on her stage-side breast. He breaks away.)* Oh-ho! That's what you're after, is it? What are we going to have . . . blue games for the guests? Hunh? Hunh?

MARTHA. *(Angry-hurt.)* You . . . prick!

GEORGE. *(A Pyrrhic victory.)* Everything in its place, Martha . . . everything in its own good time.

MARTHA. *(An unspoken epithet.)* You . . .

GEORGE. *(Over to Nick, who still has the gun.)* Here, let me show you . . . it goes back in, like this. *(Closes the parasol, reinserts it in the gun.)*

NICK. That's damn clever.

GEORGE. (*Puts the gun down.*) Drinks now! Drinks for all! (*Takes Nick's glass without question . . . goes to Martha.*)
MARTHA. (*Still angry-hurt.*) I'm not finished.
HONEY. (*As George puts out his hand for her glass.*) Oh, I think I need something. (*He takes her glass, moves back to the portable bar.*)
NICK. Is that Japanese?
GEORGE. Probably.
HONEY. (*To Martha.*) I was never so frightened in my life. Weren't you frightened? Just for a second?
MARTHA. (*Smothering her rage at George.*) I don't remember.
HONEY. Ohhhh, now . . . I bet you were. • •
GEORGE. Did you really think I was going to kill you, Martha?
MARTHA. (*Dripping contempt.*) You? . . . Kill me? . . . That's a laugh.
GEORGE. Well, now, I might . . . some day.
MARTHA. Fat chance.
NICK. (*As George hands him his drink.*) Where's the john?
GEORGE. Through the hall there . . . and down to your left.
HONEY. Don't you come back with any guns, or anything, now.
NICK. (*Laughs.*) Oh, no.
MARTHA. You don't need any props, do you, baby?
NICK. Unh-unh.
MARTHA. (*Suggestive.*) I'll bet not. No fake Jap gun for you, eh?
NICK. (*Smiles at Martha. Then, to George, indicating a side table near the hall.*) May I leave my drink here?
GEORGE. (*As Nick exits without waiting for a reply.*) Yeah . . . sure . . . why not? We've got half-filled glasses everywhere in the house, wherever Martha forgets she's left them . . . in the linen closet, on the edge of the bathtub. . . . I even found one in the freezer, once.
MARTHA. (*Amused in spite of herself.*) You did not!
GEORGE. Yes I did.
MARTHA. (*Ibid.*) You did *not!*
GEORGE. (*Giving Honey her brandy.*) Yes I did. (*To Honey.*) Brandy doesn't give you a hangover?
HONEY. I never mix. And then, I don't drink very much, either.
GEORGE. (*Grimaces behind her back.*) Oh . . . that's good.

Your . . . your husband was telling. me all about the . . . chromosomes.

MARTHA. (*Ugly.*) The what?

GEORGE. The chromosomes, Martha . . . the genes, or whatever they are. (*To Honey.*) You've got quite a . . . terrifying husband.

HONEY. (*As if she's being joshed.*) Ohhhhhhhhh . . .

GEORGE. No, really. He's quite terrifying, with his chromosomes, and all.

MARTHA. He's in the Math Department.

GEORGE. No, Martha . . . he's a biologist.

MARTHA. (*Her voice rising.*) He's in the *Math* Department!

HONEY. (*Timidly.*) Uh . . . biology.

MARTHA. (*Unconvinced.*) Are *you* sure?

HONEY. (*With a little giggle.*) Well, I ought to. (*Then as an afterthought.*) Be.

MARTHA. (*Grumpy.*) I suppose *so.* I don't know who said he was in the Math Department.

GEORGE. You did, Martha.

MARTHA. (*By way of irritable explanation.*) Well, I can't be expected to remember *everything.* I meet fifteen new teachers and their goddamn wives . . . present company outlawed, of course . . . (*Honey nods, smiles sillily.*) . . . and I'm supposed to remember *everything.* (*Pause.*) So? He's a biologist. Good for him. Biology's even better. It's less . . . abstruse.

GEORGE. Abstract.

MARTHA. ABSTRUSE! In the sense of recondite. (*Sticks her tongue out at George.*) Don't you tell me words. Biology's even better. It's . . . right at the *meat* of things. (*Nick reenters.*) You're right at the meat of things, baby.

NICK. (*Taking his drink from the side table.*) Oh?

HONEY. (*With that giggle.*) They thought you were in the Math Department.

NICK. Well, maybe I ought to be.

MARTHA. You stay right where you ˜re . . . you stay right at the . . . *meat* of things.

GEORGE. You're obsessed with that phrase, Martha. . . . It's ugly.

MARTHA. (*Ignoring George . . . to Nick.*) You stay right there. (*Laughs.*) Hell, you can take over the History Department just as easy from there as anywhere else. God knows, somebody's going to take over the History Department, some day, and it ain't going to be Georgie-boy, there . . . that's for sure. Are ya, swampy . . . are ya, Hunh?

GEORGE. In my mind, Martha, you are buried in cement, right up to your neck. (Martha giggles.) No . . . right up to your nose . . . that's much quieter.

MARTHA. (To Nick.) Georgie-boy, here, says you're terrifying. Why are you terrifying?

NICK. (With a small smile.) I didn't know I was.

HONEY. (A little thickly.) It's because of your chromosomes, dear.

NICK. Oh, the chromosome business. . . .

MARTHA. (To Nick.) What's all this about chromosomes?

NICK. Well, chromosomes are . . .

MARTHA. I know what chromosomes are, sweetie, I love 'em.

NICK. Oh . . . Well, then.

GEORGE. Martha eats them . . . for breakfast . . . she sprinkles them on her cereal. (To Martha, now.) It's very simple, Martha, this young man is working on a system whereby chromosomes can be altered . . . well not all by himself—he probably has one or two co-conspirators—the genetic makeup of a sperm cell changed, reordered . . . to order, actually . . . for hair and eye color, stature, potency . . . I imagine . . . hairiness, features, health . . . and mind. Most important . . . Mind. All imbalances will be corrected, sifted out . . . propensity for various diseases will be gone, longevity assured. We will have a race of men . . . test-tube-bred . . . incubator-born . . . superb and sublime.

MARTHA. (Impressed.) Hunh!

HONEY. How exciting!

GEORGE. But! Everyone will tend to be rather the same. . . . Alike. Everyone . . . and I'm sure I'm not wrong here . . . will tend to look like this young man here.

MARTHA. That's not a bad idea.

NICK. (Impatient.) All right, now. . . .

GEORGE. It will, on the surface of it, be all rather pretty . . . quite jolly. But of course there will be a dank side to it, too. A certain amount of regulation will be necessary . . . uh . . . for the experiment to succeed. A certain number of sperm tubes will have to be cut.

MARTHA. Hunh! . . .

GEORGE. Millions upon millions of them . . . millions of tiny little slicing operations that will leave just the smallest scar, on the underside of the scrotum (*Martha laughs.*) but which will assure the sterility of the imperfect . . . the ugly, the stupid . . . the . . . unfit.

NICK. (*Grimly.*) Now look . . . !

GEORGE. . . . with this, we will have, in time, a race of glorious men.

MARTHA. Hunh!

GEORGE. I suspect we will not have much music, much painting, but we will have a civilization of men, smooth, blond, and right at the middleweight limit.

MARTHA. Awww. . . .

GEORGE. . . . a race of scientists and mathematicians, each dedicated to and working for the greater glory of the super-civilization.

MARTHA. Goody.

GEORGE. There will be a certain . . . loss of liberty, I imagine, as a result of this experiment . . . but diversity will no longer be the goal. Cultures and races will eventually vanish . . . the ants will take over the world.

NICK. Are you finished?

GEORGE. (*Ignoring him.*) And I, naturally, am rather opposed to all this. History, which is my field . . . history, of which I am one of the most famous bogs. . . .

MARTHA. Ha, ha, HA!

GEORGE. . . . will lose its glorious variety and unpredictability. I, and with me the . . . the surprise, the multiplexity, the sea-changing rhythm of . . . history, will be eliminated. There will be order and constancy . . . and I am unalterably opposed to it. I will not give up Berlin!

MARTHA. You'll give up Berlin, sweetheart. You going to defend it with your paunch?

HONEY. I don't see what Berlin has to *do* with anything.

GEORGE. There is a saloon in West Berlin where the barstools are five feet high. And the earth . . . the floor . . . is . . . so . . . far . . . below you. I will not give up things like that. No

. . . I won't. I will fight you, young man . . . one hand on my scrotum, to be sure . . . but with my free hand I will battle you to the death.

MARTHA. (*Mocking, laughing.*) Bravo!

NICK. (*To George.*) That's right. And I am going to be the wave of the future.

MARTHA. You bet you are, baby.

HONEY. (*Quite drunk—to Nick.*) I don't see why you want to do all those things, dear. You never told me.

NICK. (*Angry.*) Oh for God's sake!

HONEY. (*Shocked.*) OH!

GEORGE. The most profound indication of a social malignancy . . . no sense of humor. None of the monoliths could take a joke. Read history. I know something about history.

NICK. (*To George, trying to make light of it all.*) You . . . you don't know much about science, do you?

GEORGE. I know something about history. I know when I'm being threatened.

MARTHA. (*Salaciously—to Nick.*) So, everyone's going to look like you, eh?

NICK. Oh, sure. I'm going to be a personal screwing machine!

MARTHA. Isn't that nice.

HONEY. (*Her hands over her ears.*) Dear, you mustn't . . . you mustn't . . . you mustn't.

NICK. (*Impatiently.*) I'm sorry, Honey.

HONEY. Such language. It's . . .

NICK. I'm sorry. All right?

HONEY. (*Pouting.*) Well . . . all right. (*Suddenly she giggles insanely, subsides. To George.*) . . . When is your son? (*Giggles again.*)

GEORGE. What?

NICK. (*Distastefully.*) Something about your son.

GEORGE. SON!

HONEY. When is . . . where is your son . . . coming home? (*Giggles.*)

GEORGE. Ohhhh. (*Too formal.*) Martha? When is our son coming home?

MARTHA. Never mind.

GEORGE. No, no . . . I want to know . . . you brought it out into the open. When is he coming home, Martha?

35

MARTHA. I said never mind. I'm sorry I brought it up.

GEORGE. Him up . . . not it. You brought *him* up. Well, more or less. When's the little bugger going to appear, hunh? I mean isn't tomorrow meant to be his birhtday, or something?

MARTHA. I don't want to talk about it!

GEORGE. (*Falsely innocent.*) But, Martha . . .

MARTHA. I DON'T WANT TO TALK ABOUT IT!

GEORGE. I'll bet you don't. (*To Honey and Nick.*) Martha does not want to talk about it . . . him. Martha is sorry she brought it up . . . him.

HONEY. (*Idiotically.*) When's the little bugger coming home? (*Giggles.*)

GEORGE. Yes, Martha . . . since you had the bad taste to bring the matter up in the first place . . . when *is* the little bugger coming home?

NICK. Honey, do you think you . . . ?

MARTHA. George talks disparagingly about the little bugger because . . . well, because he has problems.

GEORGE. The little bugger has problems? What problems has the little bugger got?

MARTHA. Not the little bugger . . . stop calling him that! You! You've got problems.

GEORGE. (*Feigned disdain.*) I've never heard of anything more ridiculous in my life.

HONEY. Neither have I!

NICK. Honey . . .

MARTHA. George's biggest problem about the little . . . ha, ha, ha, HA! . . . about our son, about our great big son, is that deep down in the private-most pit of his gut, he's not completely sure it's his own kid.

GEORGE. (*Deeply serious.*) My God, you're a wicked woman.

MARTHA. And I've told you a million times, baby . . . I wouldn't conceive with anyone but you . . . you know that, baby.

GEORGE. A deeply wicked person.

HONEY. (*Deep in drunken grief.*) My, my, my, my. Oh, my.

NICK. I'm not sure that this is a subject for . . .

GEORGE. Martha's lying. I want you to know that, right now. Martha's lying. (*Martha laughs.*) There are very few things in this world that I *am* sure of . . . national boundaries, the level

of the ocean, political allegiances, practical morality . . . none
of these would I stake my stick on any more . . . but the one
thing in this whole sinking world that I am sure of is my partnership, my chromosomological partnership in the . . . creation of
our . . . blond-eyed, blue-haired . . . son.

HONEY. Oh, I'm so glad!

MARTHA. That was a very pretty speech, George.

GEORGE. Thank you, Martha.

MARTHA. You rose to the occasion . . . good. Real good.

HONEY. Well . . . real well.

NICK. Honey . . .

GEORGE. Martha knows . . . she knows better.

MARTHA. (*Proudly.*) I know better. I been to college like everybody else.

GEORGE. Martha been to college. Martha been to a convent
when she were a little twig of a thing, too.

MARTHA. And I was an atheist. (*Uncertainly.*) I still am.

GEORGE. Not an atheist, Martha . . . a pagan. (*To Honey and
Nick.*) Martha is the only true pagan on the eastern seaboard.
(*Martha laughs.*)

HONEY. Oh, that's nice. Isn't that nice, dear?

NICK. (*Humoring her.*) Yes . . . wonderful.

GEORGE. And Martha paints blue circles around her things.

NICK. You do?

MARTHA. (*Defensively, for the joke's sake.*) Sometimes.
(*Beckoning.*) You wanna see?

GEORGE. (*Admonishing.*) Tut, tut, tut.

MARTHA. Tut, tut yourself . . . you old floozie!

HONEY. He's not a floozie . . . he can't be a floozie . . .
you're a floozie. (*Giggles.*)

MARTHA. (*Shaking a finger at Honey.*) Now you watch yourself!

HONEY. (*Cheerfully.*) All right. I'd like a nipper of brandy,
please.

NICK. Honey, I think you've had enough, now. . . .

GEORGE. Nonsense! Everybody's ready, I think. (*Takes glasses,
etc.*)

HONEY. (*Echoing George.*) Nonsense.

NICK. (*Shrugging.*) O.K.

MARTHA. (*To George.*) Our son does not have blue hair . . . or blue eyes, for that matter. He has green eyes . . . like me.

GEORGE. He has blue eyes, Martha.

MARTHA. (*Determined.*) Green.

GEORGE. (*Patronizing.*) Blue, Martha.

MARTHA. (*Ugly.*) GREEN! (*To Honey and Nick.*) He has the loveliest green eyes . . . they aren't all flaked with brown and gray, you know . . . hazel . . . they're real green . . . deep, pure green eyes . . . like mine.

NICK. (*Peers.*) Your eyes are . . . brown, aren't they?

MARTHA. Green! (*A little too fast.*) Well, in some lights they *look* brown, but they're green. Not green like his . . . more hazel. George has watery blue eyes . . . milky blue.

GEORGE. Make up your mind, Martha.

MARTHA. I was giving you the benefit of the doubt. (*Now back to the others.*) Daddy has green eyes, too.

GEORGE. He does not! Your father has tiny red eyes . . . like a white mouse. In fact, he is a white mouse.

MARTHA. You wouldn't dare say a thing like that if he was here! You're a coward!

GEORGE. (*To Honey and Nick.*) You know . . . that great shock of white hair, and those little beady red eyes . . . a great big white mouse.

MARTHA. George hates Daddy . . . not for anything Daddy's done to him, but for his own . . .

GEORGE. (*Nodding . . . finishing it for her.*) . . . inadequacies.

MARTHA. (*Cheerfully.*) That's right. You hit it . . . right on the snout. (*Seeing George exiting.*) Where do you think *you're* going?

GEORGE. We need some more booze, angel.

MARTHA. Oh. (*Pause.*) So, go.

GEORGE. (*Exiting.*) Thank you.

MARTHA. (*Seeing that George has gone.*) He's a good bartender . . . a good bar nurse. The S.O.B., he hates my father. You know that?

NICK. (*Trying to make light of it.*) Oh, come on.

MARTHA. (*Offended.*) You think I'm kidding? You think I'm joking? I never joke . . . I don't have a sense of humor. (*Almost pouting.*) I have a fine sense of the ridiculous, but no sense of humor. (*Affirmatively.*) I have no sense of humor!

HONEY. (*Happily.*) I haven't, either.

NICK. (*Half-heartedly.*) Yes, you have, Honey . . . a quiet one.

HONEY. (*Proudly.*) Thank you.

MARTHA. You want to know *why* the S.O.B. hates my father? You want me to tell you? All right . . . I will now tell you why the S.O.B. hates my father.

HONEY. (*Swinging to some sort of attention.*) Oh, good!

MARTHA. (*Sternly, to Honey.*) *Some* people feed on the calamities of others.

HONEY. (*Offended.*) They do not!

NICK. Honey . . .

MARTHA. All right! Shut up! Both of you! (*Pause.*) All right, now. Mommy died early, see, and I sort of grew up with Daddy. (*Pause—thinks.*) . . . I went away to school, and stuff, but I more or less grew up with him. Jesus, I admired that guy! I worshipped him . . . I absolutely worshipped him. I still do. And he was pretty fond of me, too . . . you know? We had a real . . . rapport going . . . a real rapport.

NICK. Yeah, yeah.

MARTHA. And Daddy built this college . . . I mean, he built it up from what it was . . . it's his whole life. He *is* the college.

NICK. Unh-hunh.

MARTHA. The college is him. You know what the endowment was when he took over, and what it is *now?* You look it up some time.

NICK. I know . . . I read about it. . . .

MARTHA. Shut up and listen . . . (*As an afterthought.*) . . . cutie. So after I got done with college and stuff, I came back here and sort of . . . sat around, for a while. I wasn't married, or anything. Welllll, I'd *been* married . . . sort of . . . for a week, my sophomore year at Miss Muff's Academy for Young Ladies . . . college. A kind of junior Lady Chatterley arrangement, as it turned out . . . the marriage. (*Nick laughs.*) He mowed the lawn at Miss Muff's, sitting up there, all naked, on a big power mower, mowing away. But Daddy and Miss Muff got together and put an end to that . . . real quick . . . annulled . . . which is a laugh . . . because theoretically you can't get an annullment if there's entrance. Ha! Anyway, so I was revirginized,

39

finished at Miss Muff's . . . where they had one less gardener's boy, and a real shame, that was . . . and I came back here and sort of sat around for a while. I was hostess for Daddy and I took care of him . . . and it was . . . nice. It was very nice.

NICK. Yes . . . yes.

MARTHA. What do you mean, yes, yes? How would you know? (*Nick shrugs helplessly.*) Lover. (*Nick smiles a little.*) And I got the idea, about then, that I'd marry into the college . . . which didn't seem to be quite as stupid as it turned out. I mean, Daddy had a sense of history . . . of . . . continuation. . . . Why don't you come over here and sit by me?

NICK. (*Indicating Honey, who is barely with it.*) I . . . don't think I . . . should. . . . I . . .

MARTHA. Suit yourself. A sense of continuation . . . history . . . and he'd always had it in the back of his mind to . . . *groom* someone to take over . . . some time, when he quit. A succession . . . you know what I mean?

NICK. Yes, I do.

MARTHA. Which is natural enough. When you've made something, you want to pass it on, to somebody. So, I was sort of on the lookout, for . . . prospects with the new men. An heir-apparent. (*Laughs.*) It wasn't Daddy's idea that I had to necessarily marry the guy. I mean, I wasn't the albatross . . . you didn't have to take me to get the prize or anything like that. It was something *I* had in the back of *my* mind. And a lot of the new men were married . . . naturally.

NICK. Sure.

MARTHA. (*With a strange smile.*) Like you, baby.

HONEY. (*A mindless echo.*) Like you, baby.

MARTHA. (*Ironically.*) But then George came along . . . along come George.

GEORGE. (*Reentering, with liquor.*) And along came George, bearing hooch. What are you doing now, Martha?

MARTHA. (*Unfazed.*) I'm telling a story. Sit down . . . you'll learn something.

GEORGE. (*Stays standing. Puts the liquor on the portable bar.*) All rightie.

HONEY. You've come back!

GEORGE. That's right.

HONEY. Dear! He's come back!

40

NICK. Yes, I see . . . I see.

MARTHA. Where was I?

HONEY. I'm *so* glad.

NICK. Shhhhh.

HONEY. (*Imitating him.*) Shhhhh.

MARTHA. Oh yeah. And along came George. That's right. WHO was young . . . intelligent . . . and . . . bushy-tailed, and . . . sort of cute . . . if you can imagine it. . . .

GEORGE. . . . and younger than you. . . .

MARTHA. . . . and younger than me. . . .

GEORGE. . . . by six years. . . .

MARTHA. . . . by six years. . . . It doesn't bother me, George. . . . And along he came, bright-eyed, into the History Department. And you know what I did, dumb cluck that I am? You know what I did? I fell for him.

HONEY. (*Dreamy.*) Oh, that's nice.

GEORGE. Yes, she did. You should have seen it. She'd sit outside of my room, on the lawn, at night, and she'd howl and claw at the turf . . . I couldn't work.

MARTHA. (*Laughs, really amused.*) I actually fell for him . . . it . . . that, there.

GEORGE. Martha's a Romantic at heart.

MARTHA. That I am. So, I actually fell for him. And the match seemed . . . practical, too. You know, Daddy was looking for someone to . . .

GEORGE. Just a minute, Martha. . . .

MARTHA. . . . take over, some time, when he was ready to . . .

GEORGE. (*Stony.*) Just a minute, Martha.

MARTHA. . . . retire, and so I thought . . .

GEORGE. STOP IT, MARTHA!

MARTHA. (*Irritated.*) Whadda you want?

GEORGE. (*Too patiently.*) I'd thought you were telling the story of our courtship, Martha . . . I didn't know you were going to start in on the other business.

MARTHA. (*So-thereish.*) Well, I am!

GEORGE. I wouldn't, if I were you.

MARTHA. Oh . . . you wouldn't? Well, you're not!

GEORGE. Now, you've already sprung a leak about you-know-what. . . .

MARTHA. (*A duck.*) What? What?

GEORGE. . . . about the apple of our eye . . . the sprout . . . the little bugger . . . (*Spits it out.*) . . . our *son* . . . and if *you* start in on this other business, I warn you, Martha, it's going to make me angry.

MARTHA. (*Laughing at him.*) Oh, it is, is it?

GEORGE. I warn you.

MARTHA. (*Incredulous.*) You *what*?

GEORGE. (*Very quietly.*) I warn you.

NICK. Do you really think we have to go through . . . ?

MARTHA. I stand warned! (*Pause . . . then, to Honey and Nick.*) So, anyway, I married the S.O.B., and I had it all planned out. . . . He was the groom . . . he was going to be groomed. He'd take over some day . . . first, he'd take over the History Department, and then, when Daddy retired, he'd take over the college . . . you know? That's the way it was supposed to be. (*To George, who is at the portable bar with his back to her.*) You getting angry, baby? Hunh? (*Now back.*) That's the way it was *supposed* to be. Very simple. And Daddy seemed to think it was a pretty good idea, too. For a while. Until he watched for a couple of years! (*To George again.*) You getting angrier? (*Now back.*) Until he watched for a couple of years and started thinking maybe it wasn't such a good idea after all . . . that maybe Georgie-boy didn't have the *stuff* . . . that he didn't have it in him!

GEORGE. (*Still with his back to them all.*) Stop it, Martha.

MARTHA. (*Viciously triumphant.*) The hell I will! You see, George didn't have much . . . push . . . he wasn't particularly . . . aggressive. In fact he was sort of a . . . (*Spits the word at George's back.*) . . . a FLOP! A great . . . big . . . fat . . . FLOP! (CRASH! *Immediately after* FLOP! *George breaks a bottle against the portable bar and stands there, still with his back to them all, holding the remains of the bottle by the neck. There is a silence, with everyone frozen. Then . . .*)

GEORGE. (*Almost crying.*) I said stop, Martha.

MARTHA. (*After considering what course to take.*) I hope that was an empty bottle, George. You don't want to waste good liquor . . . not on your salary. (*George drops the broken bottle on the floor, not moving.*) Not on an Associate Professor's salary. (*To Nick and Honey.*) I mean, he'd be . . . no good . . . at trustees'

42

dinners, fund raising. He didn't have any . . . personality, you know what I mean? Which was disappointing to Daddy, as you can imagine. So, here I am, stuck with this flop. . . .

GEORGE. (*Turning around.*) . . . don't go on, Martha. . . .

MARTHA. . . . this BOG in the History Department . . .

GEORGE. . . . don't, Martha, don't. . . .

MARTHA. (*Her voice rising to match his.*) . . . who's married to the President's daughter, who's expected to be somebody, not just some nobody, some bookworm, somebody who's so damn . . . contemplative, he can't make anything out of himself, somebody without the *guts* to make anybody proud of him . . . ALL RIGHT, GEORGE!

GEORGE. (*Under her, then covering, to drown her.*) I said, don't. All right . . . all right: (*sings.*) Who's Afraid of Virginia Woolf, Virginia Woolf, Virginia Woolf, Who's afraid of Virginia Woolf, early in the morning.

GEORGE and HONEY. (*Who joins him drunkenly.*)
Who's afraid of Virginia Woolf,
Virginia Woolf,
Virginia Woolf . . . (*etc.*)

MARTHA. STOP IT! (*A brief silence.*)

HONEY. (*Rising, moving toward the hall.*) I'm going to be sick . . . I'm going to be sick . . . I'm going to vomit. (*Exits.*)

NICK. (*Going after her.*) Oh, for God's sake! (*Exits.*)

MARTHA. (*Going after them, looks back at George, contemptuously.*) Jesus! (*Exits. George is alone on stage.*)

CURTAIN

ACT TWO

WALPURGISNACHT

George, by himself, Nick reenters.

NICK. (*After a silence.*) I . . . guess . . . she's all right. (*No answer.*) She . . . really shouldn't drink. (*No answer.*) She's . . . frail. (*No answer.*) Uh . . . slim-hipped, as you'd have it. (*George smiles vaguely.*) I'm really very sorry.
GEORGE. (*Quietly.*) Where's my little yum yum? Where's Martha?
NICK. She's making coffee . . . in the kitchen. She . . . gets sick quite easily.
GEORGE. (*Preoccupied.*) Martha? Oh no, Martha hasn't been sick a day in her life, unless you count the time she spends in the rest home. . . .
NICK. (*He, too, quietly.*) No, no; *my* wife . . . *my* wife gets sick quite easily. Your wife is Martha.
GEORGE. (*With some rue.*) Oh, yes . . . I know.
NICK. (*A statement of fact.*) She doesn't really spend any time in a rest home.
GEORGE. Your wife?
NICK. No. Yours.
GEORGE. Oh! Mine. (*Pause.*) No, no, she doesn't . . . *I* would; I mean if I were . . . her . . . she . . . *I* would. But I'm not . . . and so I don't. (*Pause.*) I'd like to, though. It gets pretty bouncy around here sometimes.
NICK. (*Coolly.*) Yes . . . I'm sure.
GEORGE. Well, you saw an example of it.
NICK. I try not to . . .
GEORGE. Get involved. Um? Isn't that right?
NICK. Yes . . . that's right.
GEORGE. I'd imagine not.
NICK. I find it . . . embarrassing.
GEORGE. (*Sarcastic.*) Oh, you do, hunh?

44

NICK. Yes. Really. Quite.

GEORGE. (*Mimicking him.*) Yes. Really. Quite. (*Then aloud, but to himself.*) IT'S DISGUSTING!

NICK. Now look! I didn't have anything . . .

GEORGE. DISGUSTING! (*Quietly, but with great intensity.*) Do you think I like having that . . . whatever-it-is . . . ridiculing me, tearing me down, in front of . . . (*Waves his hand in a gesture of contemptuous dismissal.*) YOU? Do you think I care for it?

NICK. (*Cold—unfriendly.*) Well, no . . . I don't imagine you care for it at all.

GEORGE. Oh, you don't imagine it, hunh?

NICK. (*Antagonistic.*) No . . . I don't. I don't imagine you do!

GEORGE. (*Withering.*) Your sympathy disarms me . . . your . . . your compassion makes me weep! Large, salty, unscientific tears!

NICK. (*With great disdain.*) I just don't see why you feel you have to subject other people to it.

GEORGE. I?

NICK. If you and your . . . wife . . . want to go at each other, like a couple of . . .

GEORGE. I! Why I want to!

NICK. . . . animals, I don't see why you don't do it when there aren't any . . .

GEORGE. (*Laughing through his anger.*) Why, you smug, self-righteous little . . .

NICK. (*A genuine threat.*) CAN . . . IT . . . MISTER! (*Silence.*) Just . . . watch it!

GEORGE. . . . scientist.

NICK. I've never hit an older man.

GEORGE. (*Considers it.*) Oh. (*Pause.*) You just hit younger men . . . and children . . . women . . . birds. (*Sees that Nick is not amused.*) Well, you're quite right of course. It isn't the prettiest spectacle . . . seeing a couple of middle aged types hacking away at each other, all red in the face and winded, missing half the time.

NICK. Oh, you two don't miss . . . you two are pretty good. Impressive.

GEORGE. And impressive things impress you, don't they? You're . . . easily impressed . . . sort of a . . . pragmatic idealism.

NICK. (*A tight smile.*) No, it's that sometimes I can admire

45

things that I don't admire. Now, flagellation isn't my idea of good times, but . . .

GEORGE. . . . but you can admire a good flagellator . . . a real pro.

NICK. Unh-hunh . . . yeah.

GEORGE. Your wife throws up a lot, eh?

NICK. I didn't say that. . . . I said she gets sick quite easily.

GEORGE. Oh. I thought by sick you meant . . .

NICK. Well, it's true. . . . She . . . she does throw up a lot. Once she starts . . . there's practically no stopping her. . . . I mean, she'll go right on . . . for hours. Not all the time, but . . . regularly.

GEORGE. You can tell time by her, hunh?

NICK. Just about.

GEORGE. Drink?

NICK. Sure. (*With no emotion, except the faintest distaste, as George takes his glass to the bar.*) I married her because she was pregnant.

GEORGE. (*Pause.*) Oh? (*Pause.*) But you said you didn't have any children . . . When I asked you, you said . . .

NICK. She wasn't . . . really. It was a hysterical pregnancy. She blew up, and then she went down.

GEORGE. And while she was up, you married her.

NICK. And then she went down. (*They both laugh, and are a little surprised that they do.*)

GEORGE. Uh . . . bourbon *is* right.

NICK. Uh . . . yes, bourbon.

GEORGE. (*At the bar, still.*) When I was sixteen and going to prep school, during the Punic Wars, a bunch of us used to go into New York on the first day of vacations, before we fanned out to our homes, and in the evening this bunch of us used to go to this gin mill owned by the gangster-father of one of us—for this was during the Great Experiment, or Prohibition, as it is more frequently called, and it was a bad time for the liquor lobby, but a fine time for the crooks and the cops—and we would go to this gin mill, and we would drink with the grown-ups and listen to the jazz. And one time, in the bunch of us, there was this boy who was fifteen, and he had killed his mother with a shotgun some years before—accidentally, completely accidentally, without even an unconscious motivation, I have no doubt, no doubt at

46

all—and this one evening this boy went with us, and we ordered our drinks, and when it came his turn he said, I'll have bergin . . . give me some bergin, please . . . bergin and water. Well, we all laughed . . . he was blond and he had the face of a cherub, and we all laughed, and his cheeks went red and the color rose in his neck, and the assistant crook who had taken our order told people at the next table what the boy had said, and then they laughed, and then more people were told and the laughter grew, and more people and more laughter, and no one was laughing more than us, and none of us more than the boy who had shot his mother. And soon, everyone in the gin mill knew what the laughter was about, and everyone started ordering bergin, and laughing when they ordered it. And soon, of course, the laughter became less general, but it did not subside, entirely, for a very long time, for always at this table or that someone would order bergin and a new area of laughter would rise. We drank free that night, and we were bought champagne by the management, by the gangster-father of one of us. And, of course, we suffered the next day, each of us, alone, on his train, away from New York, each of us with a grown-up's hangover . . . but it was the grandest day of my . . . youth. (*Hands Nick a drink on the word.*)

NICK. (*Very quietly.*) Thank you. What . . . what happened to the boy . . . the boy who had shot his mother?

GEORGE. I won't tell you.

NICK. All right.

GEORGE. The following summer, on a country road, with his learner's permit in his pocket and his father on the front seat to his right, he swerved the car, to avoid a porcupine, and drove straight into a large tree.

NICK. (*Faintly pleading.*) No.

GEORGE. He was not killed, of course. And in the hospital, when he was conscious and out of danger, and when they told him that his father *was* dead, he began to laugh, I have been told, and his laughter grew and he would not stop, and it was not until after they jammed a needle in his arm, not until after that, until his consciousness slipped away from him, that his laughter subsided . . . stopped. And when he was recovered from his injuries enough so that he could be moved without damage should he struggle, he was put in an asylum. That was thirty years ago.

NICK. Is he . . . still there?

GEORGE. Oh, yes. And I'm told that for these thirty years he has . . . not . . . uttered . . . one . . . sound. (*A rather long silence: five seconds, please.*) MARTHA! (*Pause.*) MARTHA!

NICK. I told you . . . she's making coffee.

GEORGE. For your hysterical wife, who goes up and down.

NICK. Went. Up and down.

GEORGE. Went. No more?

NICK. No more. Nothing.

GEORGE. (*After a sympathetic pause.*) The saddest thing about men. . . . Well, no, one of the saddest things about men is the way they age . . . some of them. Do you know what it is with insane people? Do you? . . . the quiet ones?

NICK. No.

GEORGE. They don't change . . . they don't grow old.

NICK. They must.

GEORGE. Well, eventually, probably, yes. But they don't . . . in the usual sense. They maintain a . . . a firm-skinned serenity . . . the . . . the under-use of everything leaves them . . . quite whole.

NICK. Are you recommending it?

GEORGE. No. Some things are sad, though. (*Imitates a pep-talker.*) But ya jest gotta buck up an' face 'em, 'at's all. Buck up! (*Pause.*) Martha doesn't have hysterical pregnancies.

NICK. My wife had *one*.

GEORGE. Yes. Martha doesn't have pregnancies at all.

NICK. Well, no . . . I don't imagine so . . . now. Do you have any other kids? Do you have any daughters, or anything?

GEORGE. (*As if it's a great joke.*) Do we have any *what*?

NICK. Do you have any . . . I mean, do you have only one . . . kid . . . uh . . . your son?

GEORGE. (*With a private knowledge.*) Oh no . . . just one . . . one boy . . . our son.

NICK. Well . . . (*Shrugs.*) . . . that's nice.

GEORGE. Oh ho, ho. Yes, well, he's a . . . comfort, a bean bag.

NICK. A what?

GEORGE. A bean bag. Bean bag. You wouldn't understand. (*Over-distinct.*) Bean . . . bag.

NICK. I *heard* you . . . I didn't say I was deaf . . . I said I didn't understand.

GEORGE. You didn't say that at all.

48

NICK. I meant I was *implying* I didn't understand. (*Under his breath.*) For Christ's sake!

GEORGE. You're getting testy.

NICK. (*Testy.*) I'm sorry.

GEORGE. All I said was, our son . . . the apple of our three eyes, Martha being a Cyclops . . . our son is a bean bag, and you get testy.

NICK. I'm sorry! It's late, I'm tired, I've been drinking since nine o'clock, my wife is vomiting, there's been a lot of screaming going on around here. . . .

GEORGE. And so you're testy. Naturally. Don't . . . worry about it. Anybody who comes here ends up getting . . . testy. It's expected . . . don't be upset.

NICK. (*Testy.*) I'm not upset!

GEORGE. You're testy.

NICK. Yes.

GEORGE. I'd like to set you straight about something . . . while the little ladies are out of the room . . . I'd like to set you straight about what Martha said.

NICK. I don't . . . make judgments, so there's no need, really, unless you . . .

GEORGE. Well, I want to. I know you don't like to become involved . . . I know you like to . . . preserve your scientific detachment in the face of—for lack of a better word—Life . . . and all . . . but still, I want to tell you.

NICK. (*A tight, formal smile.*) I'm a . . . guest. You go right ahead.

GEORGE. (*Mocking appreciation.*) Oh . . . well, thanks. Now! That makes me feel all warm and runny inside.

NICK. Well, if you're going to . . .

MARTHA'S VOICE. HEY!

NICK. . . . if you're going to start that kind of stuff again . . .

GEORGE. Hark! Forest sounds.

NICK. Hm?

GEORGE. Animal noises.

MARTHA. (*Sticking her head in.*) Hey!

NICK. Oh!

GEORGE. Well, here's nursie.

MARTHA. (*To Nick.*) We're sitting up . . . we're having coffee, and we'll be back in.

49

NICK. (*Not rising.*) Oh . . . is there anything I should do?

MARTHA. Nayh. You just stay here and listen to George's side of things. Bore yourself to death.

GEORGE. *Monstre!*

MARTHA. *Cochon!*

GEORGE. *Bête!*

MARTHA. *Canaille!*

GEORGE. *Putain!*

MARTHA. (*With a gesture of contemptuous dismissal.*) Yaaaahhhh! You two types amuse yourselves . . . we'll be in. (*As she goes.*) You clean up the mess you made, George?

GEORGE. (*Martha goes. George speaks to the empty hallway.*) No, Martha, I did not clean up the mess I made. I've been trying for years to clean up the mess I made.

NICK. Have you?

GEORGE. Hm?

NICK. *Have* you been trying for years?

GEORGE. (*After a long pause . . . looking at him.*) Accommodation, malleability, adjustment . . . those do seem to be in the order of things, don't they?

NICK. Don't try to put me in the same class with you!

GEORGE. (*Pause.*) Oh. (*Pause.*) No, of course not. Things are simpler with you . . . you marry a woman because she's all blown up . . . while I, in my clumsy, old-fashioned way . . .

NICK. There was more to it than that!

GEORGE. Sure! I'll bet she has money, too!

NICK. (*Looks hurt. Then, determined, after a pause.*) Yes.

GEORGE. Yes? (*Joyfully.*) YES! You mean I was right? I hit it?

NICK. Well, you see . . .

GEORGE. My God, what archery! First try, too. How about that!

NICK. You see . . .

GEORGE. There were other things.

NICK. Yes.

GEORGE. To compensate.

NICK. Yes.

GEORGE. There always are. (*Sees that Nick is reacting badly.*) No, I'm sure there are. I didn't mean to be . . . flip. There are *always* compensating factors . . . as in the case of Martha and myself. . . . Now, on the surface of it . . .

NICK. We sort of grew up together, you know. . . .

GEORGE. . . . it looks to be a kind of knock-about, drag-out affair, on the *surface* of it. . . .

NICK. We knew each other from, oh God, I don't know, when we were *six*, or something. . . .

GEORGE. . . . but somewhere back there, at the beginning of it, right when I first came to New Carthage, back then. . . .

NICK. (*With some irritation.*) I'm *sorry.*

GEORGE. Hm? Oh. No, no . . . *I'm* sorry.

NICK. No . . . it's . . . it's all right.

GEORGE. No . . . you go ahead.

NICK. No . . . please.

GEORGE. I insist. . . . You're a guest. You go first.

NICK. Well, it seems a little silly . . . now.

GEORGE. Nonsense! (*Pause.*) But if you were six, she must have been four, or something.

NICK. Maybe I was eight . . . she was six. We . . . we used to play . . . doctor.

GEORGE. That's a good healthy heterosexual beginning.

NICK. (*Laughing.*) Yup.

GEORGE. The scientist even the 1, eh?

NICK. (*Laughs.*) Yeah. And it was . . . always taken for granted . . . you know . . . by our families, and by us, too, I guess. And . . . so, we did.

GEORGE. (*Pause.*) Did what?

NICK. We got married.

GEORGE. When you were eight?

NICK. No. No, of course not. Much later.

GEORGE. I wondered.

NICK. I wouldn't say there was any . . . particular *passion* between us, even at the beginning . . . of our marriage, I mean.

GEORGE. Well, certainly no surprise, no earth-shaking discoveries, after Doctor, and all.

NICK. (*Uncertainly.*) No. . . .

GEORGE. Everything's all pretty much the same, anyway . . . in *spite* of what they say about Chinese women.

NICK. What is that?

GEORGE. Let me freshen you up. (*Takes Nick's glass.*)

NICK. Oh, thanks. After a while you don't get any drunker, do you?

GEORGE. Well, you *do* . . . but it's different . . . everything slows down . . . you get sodden . . . unless you can up-chuck . . . like your wife . . . then you can sort of start all over again.

NICK. Everybody drinks a lot here in the East. (*Thinks about it.*) Everybody drinks a lot in the middle-west, too.

GEORGE. We drink a great deal in this country, and I suspect we'll be drinking a great deal more, too . . . if we survive. We should be Arabs or Italians . . . the Arabs don't drink, and the Italians don't get drunk much, except on religious holidays. We should live on Crete, or something.

NICK. (*Sarcastically . . . as if killing a joke.*) And that, of course, would make us cretins.

GEORGE. (*Mild surprise.*) So it would. (*Hands Nick his drink.*) Tell me about your wife's money.

NICK. (*Suddenly suspicious.*) Why?

GEORGE. Well . . . don't, then.

NICK. What do you want to know about my wife's money for? (*Ugly.*) Hunh?

GEORGE. Well, I thought it would be nice.

NICK. No you didn't.

GEORGE. (*Still deceptively bland.*) All right . . . I want to know about your wife's money because . . . well, because I'm fascinated by the methodology . . . by the pragmatic accommodation by which you wave-of-the-future boys are going to take over.

NICK. You're starting in again.

GEORGE. Am I? No I'm not. Look . . . Martha has money too. I mean, her father's been robbing this place blind for years, and . . .

NICK. No, he hasn't. He has not.

GEORGE. He hasn't?

NICK. No.

GEORGE. (*Shrugs.*) Very well . . . Martha's father has *not* been robbing this place blind for years, and Martha does not have any money. O.K.?

NICK. We were talking about *my* wife's money . . . not yours.

GEORGE. O.K. . . . talk.

NICK. No. (*Pause.*) My father-in-law . . . was a man of the Lord, and he was very rich.

GEORGE. What faith?

NICK. He . . . my father-in-law . . . was called by God when he was six, or something, and he started preaching, and he baptized people, and he saved them, and he traveled around a lot, and he became pretty famous . . . not like some of them, but he became pretty famous . . . and when he died he had a lot of money.

GEORGE. God's money.

NICK. No . . . his own.

GEORGE. What happened to God's money?

NICK. He spent God's money . . . and he saved his own. He built hospitals, and he sent off Mercy ships, and he brought the outhouses indoors, and he brought the people outdoors, into the sun, and he built three churches, or whatever they were, and two of them burned down . . . and he ended up pretty rich.

GEORGE. (After considering it.) Well, I think that's very nice.

NICK. Yes. (Pause. Giggles a little.) And so, my wife's got some money.

GEORGE. But not God's money.

NICK. No. Her own.

GEORGE. Well, I think that's very nice. (Nick giggles a little.) Martha's got money because Martha's father's second wife . . . not Martha's mother, but after Martha's mother died . . . was a very old lady with warts who was very rich.

NICK. She was a witch.

GEORGE. She was a good witch, and she married the white mouse . . . (Nick begins to giggle.) . . . with the tiny red eyes . . . and he must have nibbled her warts, or something like that, because she went up in a puff of smoke almost immediately POUF!

NICK. POUF!

GEORGE. POUF! And all that was left, aside from some wart medicine, was a big fat will. . . . A peach pie, with some for the township of New Carthage, some for the college, some for Martha's daddy, and just this much for Martha.

NICK. (Quite beside himself.) Maybe . . . maybe my father-in-law and the witch with the warts should have gotten together, because he was a mouse, too.

GEORGE. (Urging Nick on.) He was?

NICK. (Breaking down.) Sure . . . he was a church mouse! (They both laugh a great deal, but it is sad laughter . . . eventually they subside, fall silent.) Your wife never mentioned a stepmother.

GEORGE. (*Considers it.*) Well . . . maybe it isn't true.

NICK. (*Narrowing his eyes.*) And maybe it is.

GEORGE. Might be . . . might not. Well, I think your story's a lot nicer . . . about your pumped-up little wife, and your father-in-law who was a priest. . . .

NICK. He was not a priest . . . he was a man of God.

GEORGE. Yes.

NICK. And my wife wasn't pumped up . . . she blew up.

GEORGE. Yes, yes.

NICK. (*Giggling.*) Get things straight.

GEORGE. I'm sorry . . . I will. I'm sorry.

NICK. O.K.

GEORGE. You realize, of course, that I've been drawing you out on this stuff, not because I'm interested in your terrible lifehood, but only because you represent a direct and pertinent threat to my lifehood, and I want to get the goods on you.

NICK. (*Still amused.*) Sure . . . sure.

GEORGE. I mean . . . I've warned you . . . you stand warned.

NICK. I stand warned. (*Laughs.*) It's you sneaky types worry me the most, you know. You ineffectual sons of bitches . . . you're the worst.

GEORGE. Yes . . . we are. Sneaky. An elbow in your steely-blue eye . . . a knee in your solid gold groin . . . we're the worst.

NICK. Yup.

GEORGE. Well, I'm glad you don't believe me. . . . I know you've got history on your side, and all. . . .

NICK. Unh-unh. *You've* got history on *your* side. . . . I've got biology on mine. History, biology.

GEORGE. I know the difference.

NICK. You don't act it.

GEORGE. No? I thought we'd decided that you'd take over the History Department first, before you took over the whole works. You know . . . a step at a time.

NICK. (*Stretching . . . luxuriating . . . playing the game.*) Nyaah . . . what I thought I'd do is . . . I'd sort of insinuate myself generally, play around for a while, find all the weak spots, shore 'em up, but with my own name plate on 'em . . . become sort of a fact, and then turn into a . . . a what . . . ?

GEORGE. An inevitability.

NICK. Exactly. . . . An inevitability. You know. . . . Take over a few courses from the older men, start some special groups for myself . . . plow a few pertinent wives. . . .

GEORGE. Now that's it! You can take over all the courses you want to, and get as much of the young elite together in the gymnasium as you like, but until you start plowing pertinent wives, you really aren't working. The way to a man's heart is through his wife's belly, and don't you forget it.

NICK. (*Playing along.*) Yeah. . . . I know.

GEORGE. And the women around here are no better than puntas —you know, South American ladies of the night. You know what they do in South America . . . in Rio? The puntas? Do you know? They hiss . . . like geese. . . . They stand around in the street and they hiss at you . . . like a bunch of geese.

NICK. Gangle.

GEORGE. Hm?

NICK. Gangle . . . gangle of geese . . . not bunch . . . gangle.

GEORGE. Well, if you're going to get all cute about it, all ornithological, it's gaggle . . . not gangle, *gaggle.*

NICK. Gaggle? Not Gangle?

GEORGE. Yes, gaggle.

NICK. (*Crestfallen.*) Oh.

GEORGE. Oh. Yes. . . . Well they stand around on the street and they hiss at you, like a bunch of geese. All the faculty wives, downtown in New Carthage, in front of the A&P, hissing away like a bunch of geese. That's the way to power—plow 'em all!

NICK. (*Still playing along.*) I'll bet you're right.

GEORGE. Well, I am.

NICK. And I'll bet your wife's the biggest goose in the gangle, isn't she . . . ? Her father president, and all.

GEORGE. You bet your historical inevitability she is!

NICK. Yessirree. (*Rubs his hands together.*) Well now, I'd just better get her off in a corner and mount her like a goddam dog, eh?

GEORGE. Why, you'd certainly better.

NICK. (*Looks at George a minute, his expression a little sick.*) You know, I almost think you're serious.

GEORGE. (*Toasting him.*) No, baby . . . *you* almost think you're serious, and it scares the hell out of you.

NICK. (*Exploding in disbelief.*) ME!

GEORGE. (*Quietly.*) Yes . . . you.

NICK. You're kidding!

GEORGE. (*Like a father.*) I wish I were. . . . I'll give you some good advice if you want me to. . . .

NICK. Good advice! From you? Oh boy! (*Starts to laugh.*)

GEORGE. You haven't learned yet. . . . Take it wherever you can get it. . . . Listen to me, now.

NICK. Come off it!

GEORGE. I'm giving you good advice, now.

NICK. Good God . . . !

GEORGE. There's quicksand here, and you'll be dragged down, just as . . .

NICK. Oh boy . . . !

GEORGE. . . . before you know it . . . sucked down. . . . (*Nick laughs derisively.*) You disgust me on principle, and you're a smug son of a bitch personally, but I'm trying to give you a survival kit. DO YOU HEAR ME?

NICK. (*Still laughing.*) I hear you. You come in loud.

GEORGE. ALL RIGHT!

NICK. Hey, Honey.

GEORGE. (*Silence. Then quietly.*) All right . . . O.K. You want to play it by ear, right? Everything's going to work out anyway, because the time-table's history, right?

NICK. Right . . . right. You just tend to your knitting, grandma. . . . I'll be O.K.

GEORGE. (*After a silence.*) I've tried to . . . tried to reach you . . . to . . .

NICK. (*Contemptuously.*) . . . make contact?

GEORGE. Yes.

NICK. (*Still.*) . . . communicate?

GEORGE. Yes. Exactly.

NICK. Aw . . . that *is* touching . . . that is . . . downright moving . . . that's what it is. (*With sudden vehemence.*) UP YOURS!

GEORGE. (*Brief pause.*) Hm?

NICK. (*Threatening.*) You heard me!

GEORGE. (*At Nick, not to him.*) You take the trouble to construct a civilization . . . to . . . to build a society, based on the principles of . . . of principle . . . you endeavor to make communicable sense out of natural order, morality out of the un-

56

natural disorder of man's mind . . . you make government and art, and realize that they are, must be, both the same . . . you bring things to the saddest of all points . . . to the point where there *is* something to lose . . . then all at once, through all the music, through all the sensible sounds of men building, attempting, comes the *Dies Irae*. And what is it? What does the trumpet sound? Up yours. I suppose there's justice to it, after all the years. . . . Up yours.

NICK. (*Brief pause . . . then applauding.*) Ha, ha! Bravo! Ha, ha! (*Laughs on. And Martha reenters, leading Honey, who is wan but smiling bravely.*)

HONEY. (*Grandly.*) Thank you . . . thank you.

MARTHA. Here we are, a little shaky, but on our feet.

GEORGE. Goodie.

NICK. What? Oh . . . oh! Hi, Honey . . . you better?

HONEY. A little bit, dear. . . . I'd better sit down, though.

NICK. Sure . . . c'mon . . . you sit by me.

HONEY. Thank you, dear.

GEORGE. (*Beneath his breath.*) Touching . . . touching.

MARTHA. (*To George.*) Well? Aren't you going to apologize?

GEORGE. (*Squinting.*) For what, Martha?

MARTHA. For making the little lady throw up, what else?

GEORGE. I did not make her throw up.

MARTHA. You most certainly did!

GEORGE. I did not!

HONEY. (*Papal gesture.*) No, now . . . no.

MARTHA. (*To George.*) Well, who do you think did . . . Sexy over there? You think he made his *own* little wife sick?

GEORGE. (*Helpfully.*) Well, you make *me* sick.

MARTHA. THAT'S DIFFERENT!

HONEY. No, now. I . . . I throw up . . . I mean, I get sick . . . occasionally, all by myself . . . without any reason.

GEORGE. Is that a fact?

NICK. You're . . . you're delicate, Honey.

HONEY. (*Proudly.*) I've always done it.

GEORGE. Like Big Ben.

NICK. (*A warning.*) Watch it!

HONEY. And the doctors say there's nothing wrong wtih me . . . organically. You know?

NICK. Of course there isn't.

HONEY. Why, just before we got married, I developed . . . appendicitis . . . or everybody *thought* it was appendicitis . . . but it turned out to be . . . it was a . . . (*Laughs briefly.*) . . . false alarm. (*George and Nick exchange glances.*)

MARTHA. (*To George.*) Get me a drink. (*George moves to the bar.*) George makes everybody sick. . . . When our son was just a little boy, he used to . . .

GEORGE. Don't, Martha. . . .

MARTHA. . . . he used to throw up all the time, because of George. . . .

GEORGE. I said, don't!

MARTHA. It got so bad that whenever George came into the room he'd start right in retching, and . . .

GEORGE. . . . the real reason (*Spits out the words.*) our son . . . used to throw up all the time, wife and lover, was nothing more complicated than that he couldn't stand you fiddling at him all the time, breaking into his bedroom with your kimono flying, fiddling at him all the time, with your liquor breath on him, and your hands all over his . . .

MARTHA. YEAH? And I suppose that's why he ran away from home twice in one month, too. (*Now to the guests.*) Twice in one month! Six times in one year!

GEORGE. (*Also to the guests.*) Our son ran away from home all the time because Martha here used to corner him.

MARTHA. (*Braying.*) I NEVER CORNERED THE SON OF A BITCH IN MY LIFE!

GEORGE. (*Handing Martha her drink.*) He used to run up to me when I'd get home, and he'd say, "Mama's always coming at me." That's what he'd say.

MARTHA. Liar!

GEORGE. (*Shrugging.*) Well, that's the way it was . . . you were always coming at him. I thought it was very embarrassing.

NICK. If you thought it was so embarrassing, what are you talking about it for?

HONEY. (*Admonishing.*) Dear . . . !

MARTHA. Yeah! (*To Nick.*) Thanks, sweetheart.

GEORGE. (*To them all.*) I didn't want to talk about him at all . . . I would have been perfectly happy not to discuss the whole subject. . . . I never want to talk about it.

MARTHA. Yes you do.

GEORGE. When we're alone, maybe.

MARTHA. We're alone!

GEORGE. Uh . . . no, Love . . . we've got guests.

MARTHA. (*With a covetous look at Nick.*) We sure have.

HONEY. Could I have a little brandy? I think I'd like a little brandy.

NICK. Do you think you should?

HONEY. Oh yes . . . yes, dear.

GEORGE. (*Moving to the bar again.*) Sure! Fill 'er up!

NICK. Honey, I don't think you . . .

HONEY. (*Petulance creeping in.*) It will steady me, *dear.* I feel a little unsteady.

GEORGE. Hell, you can't walk steady on half a bottle . . . got to do it right.

HONEY. Yes. (*To Martha.*) I love brandy . . . I really do.

MARTHA. (*Somewhat abstracted.*) Good for you.

NICK. (*Giving up.*) Well, if you think it's a good idea. . . .

HONEY. (*Really testy.*) I know what's best for me, dear.

NICK. (*Not even pleasant.*) Yes . . . I'm sure you do.

HONEY. (*George hands her a brandy.*) Oh, goodie! Thank you. (*To Nick.*) Of course I do, dear.

GEORGE. (*Pensively.*) I used to drink brandy.

MARTHA. (*Privately.*) You used to drink bergin, too.

GEORGE. (*Sharp.*) Shut up, Martha!

MARTHA. (*Her hand over her mouth in a little girl gesture.*) Oooooops.

NICK. (*Something having clicked, vaguely.*) Hm?

GEORGE. (*Burying it.*) Nothing . . . nothing.

MARTHA. (*She, too.*) You two men have it out while we were gone? George tell you his side of things? He bring you to tears, hunh?

NICK. Well . . . no. . . .

GEORGE. No, what we did, actually, was . . . we sort of danced around.

MARTHA. Oh, yeah? Cute!

HONEY. Oh, I love dancing.

NICK. He didn't mean that, Honey.

HONEY. Well, I didn't think he did! Two grown men dancing . . . heavens!

MARTHA. You mean he didn't start in on how he would have

59

amounted to something if it hadn't been for Daddy? How his high moral sense wouldn't even let him *try* to better himself? No?

NICK. (*Qualified.*) No. . . .

MARTHA. And he didn't run on about how he tried to publish a goddam book, and Daddy wouldn't let him.

NICK. A book? No.

GEORGE. Please, Martha. . . .

NICK. (*Egging her on.*) A book? What book?

GEORGE. (*Pleading.*) Please. Just a book.

MARTHA. (*Mock incredulity.*) Just a book!

GEORGE. *Please*, Martha!

MARTHA. (*Almost disappointed.*) Well, I guess you didn't get the whole sad story. What's the matter with you, George? You given up?

GEORGE. (*Calm . . . serious.*) No . . . no. It's just I've got to figure out some new way to fight you, Martha. Guerilla tactics, maybe . . . internal subversion . . . I don't know. Something.

MARTHA. Well, you figure it out, and you let me know when you do.

GEORGE. (*Cheery.*) All right, love.

HONEY. Why don't we dance? I'd love some dancing.

NICK. Honey. . . .

HONEY. I would! I'd love some dancing.

NICK. Honey. . . .

HONEY. I *want* some! I want some dancing!

GEORGE. All right . . . ! For heaven's sake . . . we'll have some dancing.

HONEY. (*All sweetness again. To Martha.*) Oh, I'm so glad . . . I just love dancing. Don't you?

MARTHA. (*With a glance at Nick.*) Yeah . . . yeah, that's not a bad idea.

NICK. (*Genuinely nervous.*) Gee.

GEORGE. Gee.

HONEY. I dance like the wind.

MARTHA. (*Without comment.*) Yeah?

GEORGE. (*Picking a record.*) Martha had her daguerreotype in the paper once . . . oh, 'bout twenty five years ago. . . . Seems she took second prize in one o' them seven-day dancin' contest things . . . biceps all bulging, holding up her partner.

MARTHA. Will you put a record on and shut up?

60

GEORGE. Certainly, love. (*To all.*) How are we going to work this? Mixed doubles?

MARTHA. Well, you certainly don't think I'm going to dance with *you,* do you?

GEORGE. (*Considers it.*) Noooooo . . . not with him around . . . that's for sure. And not with twinkle-toes here, either.

HONEY. I'll dance with anyone. . . . I'll dance by myself.

NICK. Honey. . . .

HONEY. I dance like the wind.

GEORGE. All right, kiddies . . . choose up and hit the sack. (*Music starts. . . . Second movement, Beethoven's 7th Symphony.*)

HONEY. (*Up, dancing by herself.*) De, de de *da* da, da-da de, da *da*-da de da . . . wonderful . . . !

NICK. Honey. . . .

MARTHA. All right, George . . . cut that out!

HONEY. Dum, de de da da, da-da de, dum de *da* da da. . . . Wheeeee . . . !

MARTHA. Cut it out, George!

GEORGE. (*Pretending not to hear.*) What, Martha? What?

NICK. Honey. . . .

MARTHA. (*As George turns up the volume.*) CUT IT OUT, GEORGE!

GEORGE. WHAT?

MARTHA. (*Gets up, moves quickly, threateningly, to George.*) All right, you son of a bitch.

GEORGE. (*Record off, at once. Quietly.*) What did you say, love?

MARTHA. You son of a . . .

HONEY. (*In an arrested posture.*) You stopped! Why did you stop?

NICK. Honey. . . .

HONEY. (*To Nick, snapping.*) Stop that!

GEORGE. I thought it was fitting, Martha.

MARTHA. Oh you did, hunh?

HONEY. You're always *at* me when I'm having a good time.

NICK. (*Trying to remain civil.*) I'm sorry, Honey.

HONEY. Just . . . leave me alone!

GEORGE. Well, why don't you choose Martha? (*Moves away*

from the phonograph . . . leaves it to Martha.) Martha's going
to run things . . . the little lady's going to lead the band.
HONEY. I like to dance and you don't want me to.
NICK. *I* like you to dance.
HONEY. Just . . . leave me alone. *(She sits . . . takes a drink.)*
GEORGE. Martha's going to pin on some rhythm she understands
. . . *Sacre du Printemps,* maybe. *(Moves . . . sits by Honey.)*
Hi, sexy.
HONEY. *(A little giggle-scream.)* Ooooooohhhhh!
GEORGE. *(Laughs mockingly.)* Ha, ha, ha, ha, ha. Choose it,
Martha . . . do your stuff!
MARTHA. *(Concentrating on the machine.)* You're damn right!
GEORGE. *(To Honey.)* You want to dance with me, angel-tits?
NICK. What did you call my wife?
GEORGE. *(Derisively.)* Oh boy!
HONEY. *(Petulantly.)* No! If I can't do my interpretive dance, I
don't want to dance with anyone. I'll just sit here and . . .
(Shrugs . . . drinks.)
MARTHA. *(Record on . . . a jazzy slow pop tune.)* O.K. stuff,
let's go. *(Grabs Nick.)*
NICK. Hm? Oh . . . hi.
MARTHA. Hi. *(They dance, close together, slowly.)*
HONEY. *(Pouting.)* We'll just sit here and watch.
GEORGE. That's *right!*
MARTHA. *(To Nick.)* Hey, you *are* strong, aren't you?
NICK. Unh-hunh.
MARTHA. I like that.
NICK. Unh-hunh.
HONEY. They're dancing like they've danced before.
GEORGE. It's a familiar dance . . . they both know it. . . .
MARTHA. Don't be shy.
NICK. I'm . . . not. . . .
GEORGE. *(To Honey.)* It's a very old ritual, monkey-nipples
. . . old as they come.
HONEY. I . . . I don't know what you mean. *(Nick and Martha move apart now, and dance on either side of where George and Honey are sitting; they face each other, and while their feet move but little, their bodies undulate congruently. . . . It is as if they were pressed together.)*
MARTHA. I like the way you move.

NICK. I like the way you move, too.

GEORGE. (*To Honey.*) They like the way they move.

HONEY. (*Not entirely with it.*) That's nice.

MARTHA. (*To Nick.*) I'm surprised George didn't give you his side of things.

GEORGE. (*To Honey.*) Aren't they cute?

NICK. Well, he didn't.

MARTHA. That surprises me. (*Perhaps Martha's statements are more or less in time to the music.*)

NICK. Does it?

MARTHA. Yeah . . . he usually does . . . when he gets the chance.

NICK. Well, what do you know.

MARTHA. It's really a very sad story.

GEORGE. You have ugly talents, Martha.

NICK. Is it?

MARTHA. It would make you weep.

GEORGE. Hideous gifts.

NICK. Is that so?

GEORGE. Don't encourage her.

MARTHA. Encourage me.

NICK. Go on. (*They may undulate toward each other and then move back.*)

GEORGE. I warn you . . . don't encourage her.

MARTHA. He warns you . . . don't encourage me.

NICK. I heard him . . . tell me more.

MARTHA. (*Consciously making rhymed speech.*)
> Well, Georgie-boy had lots of big ambitions
> In spite of something funny in his past. . . .

GEORGE. (*Quietly warning.*) Martha. . . .

MARTHA.
> Which Georgie-boy here turned into a novel. . . .
> His first attempt and also his last. . . .

Hey! I rhymed! I rhymed!

GEORGE. I warn you, Martha.

NICK. Yeah . . . you rhymed. Go on, go on.

MARTHA. But daddy took a look at Georgie's novel. . . .

GEORGE. You're looking for a punch in the mouth. . . . You know that, Martha.

MARTHA. Do tell! . . . and he was very shocked by what he read.

NICK. He was?

MARTHA. Yes . . . he was. . . . A novel all about a naughty boy-child. . . .

GEORGE. (*Rising.*) I will not tolerate this!

NICK (*Offhand, to George.*) Oh, can it.

MARTHA.

. . . ha, ha!

naughty boychild

who . . . uh . . . who killed his mother and his father dead.

GEORGE. STOP IT, MARTHA!

MARTHA. And Daddy said . . . Look here, I will not let you publish such a thing. . . .

GEORGE. (*Rushes to phonograph . . . rips the record off.*) That's it! The dancing's over. That's it. Go on now!

NICK. What do you think you're doing, hunh?

HONEY. (*Happily.*) Violence! Violence!

MARTHA. (*Loud: a pronouncement.*) And Daddy said . . . Look here, kid, you don't think for a second I'm going to let you publish this crap, do you? Not on your life, baby . . . not while you're teaching here. . . . You publish that goddam book and you're out . . . on your ass!

GEORGE. DESIST! DESIST!

MARTHA. Ha, ha, ha, HA!

NICK. (*Laughing.*) De . . . sist!

HONEY. Oh, violence . . . violence!

MARTHA. Why, the idea! A teacher at a respected, conservative institution like this, in a town like New Carthage, publishing a book like that? If you respect your position here, young man, young . . . whippersnapper, you'll just withdraw that manuscript. . . .

GEORGE. I will not be made mock of!

NICK. He will not be made mock of, for Christ's sake. (*Laughs. Honey joins in the laughter, not knowing exactly why.*)

GEORGE. I will not! (*All three are laughing at him. Infuriated.*) THE GAME IS OVER!

MARTHA. (*Pushing on.*) Imagine such a thing! A book about a boy who murders his mother and kills his father, and pretends it's all an accident!

HONEY. (*Beside herself with glee.*) An accident!

NICK. (*Remembering something related.*) Hey . . . wait a minute. . . .

MARTHA. (*Her own voice now.*) And you want to know the clincher? You want to know what big brave Georgie said to Daddy?

GEORGE. NO! NO! NO! NO!

NICK. Wait a minute now. . . .

MARTHA. Georgie said . . . but Daddy . . . I mean . . . ha, ha, ha, ha . . . but *Sir*, it isn't a *novel* at all. . . . (*Other voice.*) Not a novel? (*Mimicking George's voice.*) No, sir . . . it isn't a novel at all. . . .

GEORGE. (*Advancing on her.*) You will not say this!

NICK. (*Sensing the danger.*) Hey.

MARTHA. The hell I won't. Keep away from me, you bastard! (*Backs off a little . . . uses George's voice again.*) No, Sir, this isn't a novel at all . . . this is the truth . . . this really happened. . . . TO ME!

GEORGE. (*On her.*) I'LL KILL YOU! (*Grabs her by the throat. They struggle.*)

NICK. HEY! (*Comes between them.*)

HONEY. (*Wildly.*) VIOLENCE! VIOLENCE! (*George, Martha, and Nick struggle . . . yells, etc.*)

MARTHA. IT HAPPENED! TO ME! TO ME!

GEORGE. YOU SATANIC BITCH!

NICK. STOP THAT! STOP THAT!

HONEY. VIOLENCE! VIOLENCE! (*The other three struggle. George's hands are on Martha's throat. Nick grabs him, tears him from Martha, throws him on the floor. George, on the floor, Nick over him, Martha to one side, her hand on her throat.*)

NICK. That's enough now!

HONEY. (*Disappointment in her voice.*) Oh . . . oh . . . oh. . . . (*George drags himself into a chair. He is hurt, but it is more a profound humiliation than a physical injury.*)

GEORGE. (*They watch him . . . a pause. . . .*) All right . . . all right . . . very quiet now . . . we will all be . . . very quiet.

MARTHA. (*Softly, with a slow shaking of her head.*) Murderer. Mur . . . der . . . er.

NICK. (*Softly to Martha.*) O.K. now . . . that's enough. (*A brief silence. They all move around a little, self-consciously, like wrestlers flexing after a fall.)*

GEORGE. (*Composure seemingly recovered, but there is a great nervous intensity.*) Well! That's one game. What shall we do now, hunh? (*Martha and Nick laugh nervously.*) Oh come on . . . let's think of something else. We've played Humiliate the Host . . . we've gone through that one . . . what shall we do now?

NICK. Aw . . . look. . . .

GEORGE. AW LOOK! (*Whines it.*) Awww . . . looooook. (*Alert.*) I mean, come on! We must know other games, college-type types like us . . . that can't be the . . . limit of our vocabulary, can it?

NICK. I think maybe. . . .

GEORGE. Let's see now . . . what else can we do? There are other games. How about . . . how about . . . Hump the Hostess? HUNH?? How about that? How about Hump the Hostess? (*To Nick.*) You wanna play that one? You wanna play Hump the Hostess? HUNH? HUNH?

NICK. (*A little frightened.*) Calm down, now. (*Martha giggles quietly.*)

GEORGE. Or is that for later . . . mount her like a goddamn dog?

HONEY. (*Wildly toasting everybody.*) Hump the Hostess!

NICK. (*To Honey . . . sharply.*) Just shut up . . . will you? (*Honey does, her glass in mid-air.*)

GEORGE. You don't wanna play that now, hunh? You wanna save that game till later? Well, what'll we play now? We gotta play a game.

MARTHA. (*Quietly.*) Portrait of a man drowning.

GEORGE. (*Affirmatively, but to none of them.*) I am not drowning.

HONEY. (*To Nick, tearfully indignant.*) You told me to shut up!

NICK. (*Impatiently.*) I'm sorry.

HONEY. (*Between her teeth.*) No you're not.

NICK. (*To Honey, even more impatiently.*) I'm sorry.

GEORGE. (*Claps his hands together, once, loud.*) I've got it! I'll tell you what game we'll play. We're done with Humiliate the Host . . . this round, anyway . . . we're done with that . . . and we don't want to play Hump the Hostess, yet . . . not yet

66

. . . so I know what we'll play. . . . We'll play a round of Get the Guests. How about that? How about a little game of Get the Guests?

MARTHA. (*Turning away, a little disgusted.*) Jesus, George.

GEORGE. Book dropper! Child mentioner!

HONEY. I don't like these games.

NICK. Yeah. . . . I think maybe we've had enough of games, now. . . .

GEORGE. Oh, no . . . oh, no . . . we haven't. We've had only one game. . . . Now we're going to have another. You can't fly on one game.

NICK. I think maybe . . .

GEORGE. (*With great authority.*) SILENCE! (*It is respected.*) Now, how are we going to play Get the Guests?

MARTHA. For God's sake, George. . . .

GEORGE. You be quiet! (*Martha shrugs.*) I wonder . . . I wonder. (*Puzzles . . . then. . . .*) O.K.! Well . . . Martha . . . in her indiscreet way . . . well, not really indiscreet, because Martha is a naive, at heart . . . anyway, Martha told you all about my first novel. True or false? Hunh? I mean, true or false that there ever was such a thing. HA! But, Martha told you about it . . . my first novel, my . . . memory book . . . which I'd sort of preferred she hadn't, but hell, that's blood under the bridge. BUT! what she didn't do . . . what Martha didn't tell you about is she didn't tell us all about my *second* novel. (*Martha looks at him with puzzled curiosity.*) No, you didn't know about that, did you, Martha? About my second novel, true or false. True or false?

MARTHA. (*Sincerely.*) No.

GEORGE. No. (*He starts quietly but as he goes on, his tone becomes harsher, his voice louder.*) Well, it's an allegory, really—probably—but it can be read as straight, cozy prose . . . and it's all about a nice young couple who come out of the middle west. It's a bucolic you see. AND, this nice young couple comes out of the middle west, and he's blond and about thirty, and he's a scientist, a teacher, a scientist . . . and his mouse is a wifey little type who gargles brandy all the time . . . and . . .

NICK. Just a minute here. . . .

GEORGE. . . . and they got to know each other when they was

67

only teensie little types, and they used to get under the vanity table and poke around, and . . .

NICK. I said JUST A MINUTE!

GEORGE. This is my game! You played yours . . . you people. This is my game!

HONEY. (Dreamy.) I want to hear the story. I love stories.

MARTHA. George, for heaven's sake. . . .

GEORGE. AND! And Mousie's father was a holy man, see, and he ran sort of a traveling clip joint, based on Christ and all those girls, and he took the faithful . . . that's all . . . just took 'em. . . .

HONEY. (Puzzling.) This is familiar. . . .

NICK. (Voice shaking a little.) No kidding!

GEORGE. . . . and he died eventually, Mousie's pa, and they pried him open, and all sorts of money fell out. . . . Jesus money, Mary money. . . . LOOT!

HONEY. (Dreamy, puzzling.) I've heard this story before.

NICK. (With quiet intensity . . . to waken her.) Honey . . .

GEORGE. But that's in the backwash, in the early part of the book. Anyway, Blondie and his frau out of the plain states came. (Chuckles.)

MARTHA. Very funny, George. . . .

GEORGE. . . . thank you . . . and settled in a town just like nouveau Carthage here. . . .

NICK. (Threatening.) I don't think you'd better go on, mister. . . .

GEORGE. Do you not!

NICK. (Less certainly.) No. I . . . I don't think you'd better.

HONEY. I love familiar stories . . . they're the best.

GEORGE. How right you are. But Blondie was in disguise, really, all got up as a teacher, 'cause his baggage ticket had bigger things writ on it . . . H.I. HI! Historical inevitability.

NICK. There's no need for you to go any further, now. . . .

HONEY. (Puzzling to make sense out of what she is hearing.) Let them go on.

GEORGE. We shall. And he had this baggage with him, and part of this baggage was in the form of his mouse. . . .

NICK. We don't have to listen to this!

HONEY. Why not?

GEORGE. Your bride has a point. And one of the things nobody could understand about Blondie was his baggage . . . his mouse, I mean, here he was, pan-Kansas swimming champeen, or something, and he had this mouse, of whom he was solicitous to a point that faileth human understanding . . . given that she was sort of a simp, in the long run. . . .

NICK. This isn't fair of you. . . .

GEORGE. Perhaps not. Like, as I said, his mouse, she tooted brandy immodestly and spent half of her time in the upchuck. . . .

HONEY. (*Focussing.*) I know these people. . . .

GEORGE. Do you! . . . But she was a money baggage amongst other things . . . Godly money ripped from the golden teeth of the unfaithful, a pragmatic extension of the big dream . . . and she was put up with. . . .

HONEY. (*Some terror.*) I don't like this story. . . .

NICK. (*Surprisingly pleading.*) Please . . . please don't.

MARTHA. Maybe you better stop, George. . . .

GEORGE. . . . and she was put up with. . . . STOP? Ha-ha.

NICK. Please . . . please don't.

GEORGE. Beg, baby.

MARTHA. George . . .

GEORGE. . . . and . . . oh, we get a flashback here, to How They Got Married.

NICK. NO!

GEORGE. (*Triumphant.*) YES!

NICK. (*Almost whining.*) Why?

GEORGE. How They Got Married. Well, how they got married is this. . . . The Mouse got all puffed up one day, and she went over to Blondie's house, and she stuck out her puff, and she said . . . look at me.

HONEY. (*White . . . on her feet.*) I . . . don't . . . like this.

NICK. (*To George.*) Stop it!

GEORGE. Look at me . . . I'm all puffed up. Oh my goodness, said Blondie. . . .

HONEY. (*As from a distance.*) . . . and so they were married. . . .

GEORGE. . . . and so they were married. . . .

HONEY. . . . and then . . .

GEORGE. . . . and then . . .

HONEY. (*Hysteria.*) WHAT? . . . and then, WHAT?

NICK. NO! No!

GEORGE. (*As if to a baby.*) . . . and then the puff went *away* . . . like magic . . . pouf!

NICK. (*Almost sick.*) Jesus God . . .

HONEY. . . . the puff went away. . . .

GEORGE. (*Softly.*) . . . pouf.

NICK. Honey . . . I didn't mean to . . . honestly, I didn't mean to . . .

HONEY. You . . . you told them. . . .

NICK. Honey . . . I didn't mean to . . .

HONEY. (*With outlandish horror.*) You . . . told them! You told them! ooooHHHH! Oh, no, no, no, no! You couldn't have told them . . . oh, noooo!

NICK. Honey, I didn't mean to . . .

HONEY. (*Grabbing at her belly.*) Ohhhhh . . . nooooo.

NICK. Honey . . . baby . . . I'm sorry . . . I didn't mean to . . .

GEORGE. (*Abruptly and with some disgust.*) And that's how you play Get the Guests.

HONEY. I'm going to . . . I'm going to be . . . sick . . .

GEORGE. Naturally!

NICK. Honey . . .

HONEY. (*Hysterical.*) Leave me alone . . . I'm going . . . to . . . be . . . sick. (*She runs out of the room.*)

MARTHA. (*Shaking her head, watching Honey's retreating form.*) God Almighty.

GEORGE. (*Shrugging.*) The patterns of history.

NICK. (*Quietly shaking.*) You shouldn't have done that . . . you shouldn't have done that at all.

GEORGE. (*Calmly.*) I hate hypocrisy.

NICK. That was cruel . . . and vicious. . . .

GEORGE. . . . she'll get over it. . . .

NICK. . . . and damaging . . . !

GEORGE. . . . she'll recover. . . .

NICK. DAMAGING!! TO ME!!

GEORGE. (*With wonder.*) To you!

NICK. TO ME!!

GEORGE. To you!!

NICK. YES!!

GEORGE. Oh beautiful . . . beautiful. By God, you gotta have a swine to show you where the truffles are. (*So calmly.*) Well, you just rearrange your alliances, boy. You just pick up the pieces where you can . . . you just look around and make the best of things . . . you scramble back up on your feet.

MARTHA. (*Quietly, to Nick.*) Go look after your wife.

GEORGE. Yeah . . . go pick up the pieces and plan some new strategy.

NICK. (*To George, as he moves toward the hall.*) You're going to regret this.

GEORGE. Probably. I regret everything.

NICK. I mean, I'm going to make you regret this.

GEORGE. (*Softly.*) No doubt. Acute embarrassment, eh?

NICK. I'll play the charades like you've got 'em set up. . . . I'll play in your language. . . . I'll be what you say I am.

GEORGE. You are already . . . you just don't know it.

NICK. (*Shaking within.*) No . . . no. Not really. But I'll *be* it, mister. . . . I'll show you something come to life you'll wish you hadn't set up.

GEORGE. Go clean up the mess.

NICK. (*Quietly . . . intensely.*) You just wait, mister. (*He exits. Pause. George smiles at Martha.*)

MARTHA. Very good, George.

GEORGE. Thank you, Martha.

MARTHA. Really good.

GEORGE. I'm glad you liked it.

MARTHA. I mean. . . . You did a good job . . . you really fixed it.

GEORGE. Unh-hunh,

MARTHA. It's the most . . . life you've shown in a long time.

GEORGE. You bring out the best in me, baby.

MARTHA. Yeah . . . pigmy hunting!

GEORGE. PIGMY!

MARTHA. You're really a bastard.

GEORGE. I? I?

MARTHA. Yeah . . . you.

GEORGE. Baby, if quarterback there is a pigmy, you've certainly changed your style. What are you after now . . . giants?

MARTHA. You make me sick.

GEORGE. It's perfectly all right for you. . . . I mean, you can make your own rules . . . you can go around like a hopped-up

Arab, slashing away at everything in sight, scarring up half the world if you want to. But somebody else try it . . . no sir! MARTHA. You miserable . . .

GEORGE. (*Mocking.*) Why baby, I did it all for you. I thought you'd like it, sweetheart . . . it's sort of to your taste . . . blood, carnage and all. Why, I thought you'd get all excited . . . sort of heave and pant and come running at me, your melons bobbling.

MARTHA. You've really screwed up, George.

GEORGE. (*Spitting it out.*) Oh, for God's sake, Martha!

MARTHA. I mean it . . . you really have.

GEORGE. (*Barely contained anger now.*) You can sit there in that chair of yours, you can sit there with the gin running out of your mouth, and you can humiliate me, you can tear me apart . . . ALL NIGHT . . . and that's perfectly all right . . . that's O.K. . . .

MARTHA. YOU CAN STAND IT!

GEORGE. I CANNOT STAND IT!

MARTHA. YOU CAN STAND IT!! YOU MARRIED ME FOR IT!! (*A silence.*)

GEORGE. (*Quietly.*) That is a desperately sick lie.

MARTHA. DON'T YOU KNOW IT, EVEN YET?

GEORGE. (*Shaking his hand.*) Oh . . . Martha.

MARTHA. My arm has gotten tired whipping you.

GEORGE. (*Stares at her in disbelief.*) You're mad.

MARTHA. For twenty-three years!

GEORGE. You're deluded . . . Martha, you're deluded.

MARTHA. IT'S NOT WHAT I'VE WANTED!

GEORGE. I thought at least you were . . . on to yourself. I didn't know. I . . . didn't know.

MARTHA. (*Anger taking over.*) I'm on to myself.

GEORGE. (*As if she were some sort of bug.*) No . . . no . . . you're . . . sick.

MARTHA. (*Rises—screams.*) I'LL SHOW YOU WHO'S SICK!

GEORGE. All right, Martha . . . you're going too far.

MARTHA. (*Screams again.*) I'LL SHOW YOU WHO'S SICK. I'LL SHOW YOU.

GEORGE. (*He shakes her.*) Stop it! (*Pushes her back in her chair.*) Now, stop it!

MARTHA. (*Calmer.*) I'll show you who's sick. (*Calmer.*) Boy,

you're really having a field day, hunh? Well, I'm going to finish
you . . before I'm through with you. . . .
GEORGE. . . . you and the quarterback . . . you both gonna
finish me . . . ?
MARTHA. . . . before I'm through with you you'll wish you'd
died in that automobile, you bastard.
GEORGE. (*Emphasizing with his forefinger.*) And you'll wish
you'd never mentioned our son!
MARTHA. (*Dripping contempt.*) You . . .
GEORGE. Now, I said I warned you.
MARTHA. I'm impressed.
GEORGE. I warned you not to go too far.
MARTHA. I'm just beginning.
GEORGE. (*Calmly, matter-of-factly.*) I'm numbed enough . .
and I don't mean by liquor, though maybe that's been part of the
process—a gradual, over-the-years going to sleep of the brain
cells—I'm numbed enough, now, to be able to take you when
we're alone. I don't listen to you . . . or when I *do* listen to
you, I sift everything, I bring everything down to reflex response, so I don't really *hear* you, which is the only way to man-
age it. But you've taken a new tack, Martha, over the past couple
of centuries—or however long it's been I've lived in this house
with you—that makes it just too much . . . too much. I don't
mind your dirty underthings in public . . . well, I *do* mind, but
I've reconciled myself to that . . . but you've moved bag and
baggage into your own fantasy world now, and you've started
playing variations on your own distortions, and, as a result . . .
MARTHA. Nuts!
GEORGE. Yes . . . you have.
MARTHA. Nuts!
GEORGE. Well, you can go on like that as long as you want to.
And, when you're done . . .
MARTHA. Have you ever listened to your sentences, George?
Have you ever listened to the way you talk? You're so frigging
. . . convoluted . . . that's what you are. You talk like you were
writing one of your stupid papers.
GEORGE. Actually, I'm rather worried about you. About your
mind.
MARTHA. Don't you worry about my mind, sweetheart!
GEORGE. I think I'll have you committed.

MARTHA. You WHAT?

GEORGE. (Quietly . . . distinctly.) I think I'll have you committed.

MARTHA. (Breaks into long laughter.) Oh baby, aren't you something!

GEORGE. I've got to find some way to really get at you.

MARTHA. You've got at me, George . . . you don't have to do anything. Twenty-three years of you has been quite enough.

GEORGE. Will you go quietly, then?

MARTHA. You know what's happened, George? You want to know what's really happened? (Snaps her fingers.) It's snapped, finally. Not me . . . it. The whole arrangement. You can go along . . . forever, and everything's . . . manageable. You make all sorts of excuses to yourself . . . you know . . . this is life . . . the hell with it . . . maybe tomorrow he'll be dead . . . maybe tomorrow you'll be dead . . . all sorts of excuses. But then, one day, one night, something happens . . . and SNAP! It breaks. And you just don't give a damn any more. I've tried with you, baby . . . really, I've tried.

GEORGE. Come off it, Martha.

MARTHA. I've tried . . . I've really tried.

GEORGE. (With some awe.) You're a monster . . . you are.

MARTHA. I'm loud, and I'm vulgar, and I wear the pants in this house because somebody's got to, but I am not a monster. I am not.

GEORGE. You're a spoiled, self-indulgent, willful, dirty-minded, liquor-ridden . . .

MARTHA. SNAP! It went snap. Look, I'm not going to try to get through to you any more. . . . I'm not going to try. There was a second back there, maybe, there was a second, just a second, when I could have gotten through to you, when maybe we could have cut through all this crap. But that's past, and now I'm not going to try.

GEORGE. Once a month, Martha! I've gotten used to it . . . once a month and we get misunderstood Martha, the good-hearted girl underneath the barnacles, the little Miss that the touch of kindness'd bring to bloom again. And I've believed it more times than I want to remember, because I don't want to think I'm that much of a sucker. I don't believe you . . . I just

74

don't believe you. There is no moment . . . there is no moment any more when we could . . . come together.

MARTHA. (*Armed again.*) Well, maybe you're right, baby. You can't come together with nothing, and you're nothing! SNAP! It went snap tonight at Daddy's party. (*Dripping contempt, but there is fury and loss under it.*) I sat there at Daddy's party, and I watched you . . . I watched you sitting there, and I watched the younger men around you, the men who were going to go somewhere. And I sat there and I watched you, and *you* weren't *there!* And it snapped! It finally snapped! And I'm going to howl it out, and I'm not going to give a damn what I do, and I'm going to make the damned biggest explosion you ever heard.

GEORGE. (*Very pointedly.*) You try it and I'll beat you at your own game.

MARTHA. (*Hopefully.*) Is that a threat, George? Hunh?

GEORGE. That's a threat, Martha.

MARTHA. (*Fake-spits at him.*) You're going to get it, baby.

GEORGE. Be careful, Martha . . . I'll rip you to pieces.

MARTHA. You aren't man enough . . . you haven't got the guts.

GEORGE. Total war?

MARTHA. Total. (*Silence. They both seem relieved . . . elated. Nick reenters.*)

NICK. (*Brushing his hands off.*) Well . . . she's . . . resting.

GEORGE. (*Quietly amused at Nick's calm, off-hand manner.*) Oh?

MARTHA. Yeah? She all right?

NICK. I think so . . . now. I'm . . . terribly sorry, . . .

MARTHA. Forget about it.

GEORGE. Happens all the time around here.

NICK. She'll be all right.

MARTHA. She lying down? You put her upstairs? On a bed?

NICK. (*Making himself a drink.*) Well, no, actually. Uh . . . may I? She's . . . in the bathroom . . . on the bathroom floor . . . she's lying there.

GEORGE. (*Considers it.*) Well . . . that's not very nice.

NICK. She likes it. She says it's . . . cool.

GEORGE. Still, I don't think . . .

MARTHA. (*Overruling him.*) If she wants to lie on the bathroom floor, let her. (*To Nick, seriously.*) Maybe she'd be more comfortable in the tub?

75

NICK. (*He, too, seriously.*) No, she says she likes the floor . . .
she took up the mat, and she's lying on the tiles. She . . . she
lies on the floor a lot . . . she really does.

MARTHA. (*Pause.*) Oh.

NICK. She . . . she gets lots of headaches and things, and she
always lies on the floor. (*To George.*) Is there . . . ice?

GEORGE. What?

NICK. Ice. Is there ice?

GEORGE. (*As if the word were unfamiliar to him.*) Ice?

NICK. Ice. Yes.

MARTHA. Ice.

GEORGE. (*As if he suddenly understood.*) Ice!

MARTHA. Attaboy.

GEORGE. (*Without moving.*) Oh, yes . . . I'll get some.

MARTHA. Well, go. (*Mugging . . . to Nick.*) Besides, we want
to be alone.

GEORGE. (*Moving to take the bucket.*) I wouldn't be surprised,
Martha . . . I wouldn't be surprised.

MARTHA. (*As if insulted.*) Oh, you wouldn't, hunh?

GEORGE. Not a bit, Martha.

MARTHA. (*Violent.*) NO?

GEORGE. (*He too.*) NO! (*Quietly again.*) You'll try anything,
Martha. (*Picks up the ice bucket.*)

NICK. (*To cover.*) Actually, she's very . . . frail, and . . .

GEORGE. . . . slim-hipped.

NICK. (*Remembering.*) Yes . . . exactly.

GEORGE. (*At the hallway . . . not kindly.*) That why you don't
have any kids? (*He exits.*)

NICK. (*To George's retreating form.*) Well, I don't know that
that's . . . (*Trails off.*) . . . if that has anything to do with any
. . . thing.

MARTHA. Well, if it does, who cares? Hunh?

NICK. Pardon? (*Martha blows him a kiss. Nick, still concerned
with George's remark.*) I . . . what? . . . I'm sorry.

MARTHA. I said . . . (*Blows him another kiss.*)

NICK. (*Uncomfortable.*) Oh . . . yes.

MARTHA. Hey . . . hand me a cigarette . . . lover. (*Nick
fishes in his pocket.*) That's a good boy. (*He gives her one.*) Unh
. . . thanks. (*He lights it for her. As he does, she slips her hand
between his legs, somewhere between the knee and the crotch,*

76

bringing her hand around to the outside of his leg.) **Ummmm-mmmm.** *(He seems uncertain, but does not move. She smiles, moves her hand a little.)* Now, for being such a good boy, you can give me a kiss. C'mon.
NICK. *(Nervously.)* Look . . . I don't think we should. . . .
MARTHA. C'mon, baby . . . a friendly kiss.
NICK. *(Still uncertain.)* Well . . .
MARTHA. . . . you won't get hurt, little boy. . . .
NICK. . . . not so little. . . .
MARTHA. I'll bet you're not. C'mon. . . .
NICK. *(Weakening.)* But what if he should come back in, and . . . or . . . ?
MARTHA. *(All the while her hand is moving up and down his leg.)* George? Don't worry about him. Besides, who could object to a friendly little kiss? It's all in the faculty. *(They both laugh, quietly . . . Nick a little nervously.)* We're a close-knit family here . . . Daddy always says so. . . . Daddy wants us to get to know each other . . . that's what he had the party for tonight. So c'mon . . . let's get to know each other a little bit.
NICK. It isn't that I don't want to . . . believe me. . . .
MARTHA. You're a scientist, aren't you? C'mon . . . make an experiment . . . make a little experiment. Experiment on old Martha.
NICK. *(Giving in.)* . . . not very old. . . .
MARTHA. That's right, not very old, but lots of good experience . . . lots of it.
NICK. I'll . . . I'll bet.
MARTHA. *(As they draw slowly closer.)* It'll be a nice change for you, too.
NICK. Yes, it would.
MARTHA. And you could go back to your little wife all refreshed.
NICK. *(Closer . . . almost whispering.)* She wouldn't know the difference.
MARTHA. Well, nobody else's going to know, either. *(They come together. What might have been a joke rapidly becomes serious, with Martha urging it in that direction. There is no frenetic quality, but rather a slow, continually involving intertwining. Perhaps Martha is still more or less in her chair, and Nick is sort of beside and on the chair. George enters . . . stops . . . watches*

77

a moment . . . smiles . . . laughs silently, nods his head, turns, exits, without being noticed. Nick, who has already had his hand on Martha's breast, now puts his hand inside her dress. Martha, slowing him down.) Hey . . . hey. Take it easy, boy. Down, baby. Don't rush it, hunh?

NICK. *(His eyes still closed.)* Oh, c'mon, now. . . .

MARTHA. *(Pushing him away.)* Unh-unh. Later, baby . . . later.

NICK. I told you . . . I'm a biologist.

MARTHA. *(Soothing him.)* I know. I can tell. Later, hunh? *(George is heard off-stage, singing "Who's afraid of Virginia Woolf?" Martha and Nick go apart, Nick wiping his mouth Martha checking her clothes. Safely later, George reenters with the ice bucket.)*

GEORGE.

> . . . of Virginia Woolf,
> Virginia Woolf,
> Virginia . . .

. . . ah! Here we are . . . ice for the lamps of China, Manchuria thrown in. *(To Nick.)* You better watch those yellow bastards, my love . . . they aren't amused. Why don't you come on over to our side, and we'll blow the hell out of 'em. Then we can split up the money between us and be on Easy Street. What d'ya say?

NICK. *(Not at all sure what is being talked about.)* Well . . . sure. Hey! Ice!

GEORGE. *(With hideously false enthusiasm.)* Right! *(Now to Martha, purring.)* Hello, Martha . . . my dove. . . . You look . . . radiant.

MARTHA. *(Off-hand.)* Thank you.

GEORGE. *(Very cheerful.)* Well now, let me see. I've got the ice. . . .

MARTHA. . . . gotten . . .

GEORGE. *Got*, Martha. Got is perfectly correct . . . it's just a little . . . archaic, like you.

MARTHA. *(Suspicious.)* What are you so cheerful about?

GEORGE. *(Ignoring the remark.)* Let's see now . . . I've got the ice. Can I make someone a drink? Martha, can I make you a drink?

MARTHA. *(Bravura.)* Yeah, why not?

78

GEORGE. (*Taking her glass.*) Indeed . . . why not? (*Examines the glass.*) Martha! You've been nibbling away at the glass.

MARTHA. I have not!

GEORGE. (*To Nick, who is at the bar.*) I see you're making your own, which is fine . . . fine. I'll just hootch up Martha, here, and then we'll be all set.

MARTHA. (*Suspicious.*) All set for what?

GEORGE. (*Pause . . . considers.*) Why, I don't know. We're having a party, aren't we? (*To Nick, who has moved from the bar.*) I passed your wife in the hall. I mean, I passed the john and I looked in on her. Peaceful . . . so peaceful. Sound asleep . . . and she's actually . . . sucking her thumb.

MARTHA. Awwwwww!

GEORGE. Rolled up like a fetus, sucking away.

NICK. (*A little uncomfortably.*) I suppose she's all right.

GEORGE. (*Expansively.*) Of course she is! (*Hands Martha her drink.*) There you are.

MARTHA. (*Still on her guard.*) Thanks.

GEORGE. And now one for me. It's my turn.

MARTHA. Never, baby . . . it's never your turn.

GEORGE. (*Too cheerful.*) Oh, now, I wouldn't say that, Martha.

MARTHA. You moving on the principle the worm turns? Well, the worm part's O.K. . . . cause that fits you fine, but the turning part . . . unh-unh! You're in a straight line, buddy-boy, and it doesn't lead anywhere . . . (*A vague afterthought.*) . . . except maybe the grave.

GEORGE. (*Chuckles, takes his drink.*) Well, you just hold that thought, Martha . . . hug it close . . . run your hands over it. Me, I'm going to sit down . . . if you'll excuse me. . . . I'm going to sit down over there and read a book. (*He moves to a chair facing away from the center of the room, but not too far from the front door.*)

MARTHA. You're gonna do what?

GEORGE. (*Quietly, distinctly.*) I am going to read a book. Read. Read. Read? You've heard of it? (*Picks up a book.*)

MARTHA. (*Standing.*) Whaddya mean you're gonna read? What's the matter with you?

GEORGE. (*Too calmly.*) There's nothing the matter with me, Martha. . . . I'm going to read a book. That's all.

MARTHA. (*Oddly furious.*) We've got company!

79

GEORGE. (*Over-patiently.*) I know, my dear . . . (*Looks at his watch.*) . . . but . . . it's after four o'clock, and I always read around this time. Now, you . . . (*Dismisses her with a little wave.*) . . . go about your business. . . . I'll sit here very quietly. . . .

MARTHA. You read in the afternoon! You read at four o'clock in the afternoon . . . you don't read at four o'clock in the morning! Nobody reads at four o'clock in the morning!

GEORGE. (*Absorbing himself in his book.*) Now, now, now.

MARTHA. (*Incredulously, to Nick.*) He's going to read a book. . . . The son of a bitch is going to read a book!

NICK. (*Smiling a little.*) So it would seem. (*Moves to Martha, puts his arm around her waist. George cannot see this, of course.*)

MARTHA. (*Getting an idea.*) Well, we can amuse ourselves, can't we?

NICK. I imagine so.

MARTHA. We're going to amuse ourselves, George.

GEORGE. (*Not looking up.*) Unh-hunh. That's nice.

MARTHA. You might not like it.

GEORGE. (*Never looking up.*) No, no, now . . . you go right ahead . . . you entertain your guests.

MARTHA. I'm going to entertain myself, too.

GEORGE. Good . . . good.

MARTHA. Ha, ha. You're a riot, George.

GEORGE. Unh-hunh.

MARTHA. Well, I'm a riot, too, George.

GEORGE. Yes you are, Martha. (*Nick takes Martha's hand, pulls her to him. They stop for a moment, then kiss, not briefly.*)

MARTHA. (*After.*) You know what I'm doing, George?

GEORGE. No, Martha . . . what are you doing?

MARTHA. I'm entertaining. I'm entertaining one of the guests. I'm necking with one of the guests.

GEORGE. (*Seemingly relaxed and preoccupied, never looking.*) Oh, that's nice. Which one?

MARTHA. (*Livid.*) Oh, by God you're funny. (*Breaks away from Nick . . . moves into George's side-line of vision by herself. Her balance is none too good, and she bumps into or brushes against the door chimes by the door. They chime.*)

GEORGE. Someone at the door, Martha.

MARTHA. Never mind that. I said I was necking with one of the guests.

GEORGE. Good . . . good. You go right on.

MARTHA. (*Pauses . . . not knowing quite what to do.*) Good?

GEORGE. Yes, good . . . good for you.

MARTHA. (*Her eyes narrowing, her voice becoming hard.*) Oh, I see what you're up to, you lousy little . . .

GEORGE. I'm up to page a hundred and . . .

MARTHA. Cut it! Just cut it out! (*She hits against the door chimes again; they chime.*) Goddam bongs.

GEORGE. They're chimes, Martha. Why don't you go back to your necking and stop bothering me? I want to read.

MARTHA. Why you, miserable . . . I'll show *you*.

GEORGE. (*Swings around to face her . . . says, with great loathing.*) No . . . show him, Martha . . . he hasn't seen it. *Maybe* he hasn't seen it. (*Turns to Nick.*) You haven't seen it yet, have you?

NICK. (*Turning away, a look of disgust on his face.*) I . . . I have no respect for you.

GEORGE. And none for yourself, either. . . . (*Indicating Martha.*) I don't know what the younger generation's coming to.

NICK. You don't . . . you don't even . . .

GEORGE. Care? You're quite right. . . . I couldn't care less. So, you just take this bag of laundry here, throw her over your shoulder, and . . .

NICK. You're disgusting.

GEORGE. (*Incredulous.*) Because you're going to hump Martha, *I'm* disgusting? (*He breaks down in ridiculous laughter.*)

MARTHA. (*To George.*) You Mother! (*To Nick.*) Go wait for me, hunh? Go wait for me in the kitchen. (*But Nick does not move. Martha goes to him, puts her arms around him.*) C'mon, baby . . . please. Wait for me . . . in the kitchen . . . be a good baby. (*Nick takes her kiss, glares at George . . . who has turned his back again . . . and exits. Martha swings around to George.*) Now you listen to me. . . .

GEORGE. I'd rather read, Martha, if you don't mind. . . .

MARTHA. (*Her anger has her close to tears, her frustration to fury.*) Well, I do mind. Now, you pay attention to me! You come off this kick you're on, or I swear to God I'll do it. I swear

81

to God I'll follow that guy into the kitchen, and then I'll take him upstairs, and . . .

GEORGE. (*Swinging around to her again . . . loud . . . loathing.*) SO WHAT, MARTHA?

MARTHA. (*Considers him for a moment . . . then, nodding her head, backing off slowly.*) O.K. . . . O.K. . . . You asked for it . . . and you're going to get it

GEORGE (*Softly, sadly.*) Lord, Martha, if you want the boy that much . . . have him . . . but do it honestly, will you? Don't cover it over with all this . . . all this . . . footwork.

MARTHA. (*Hopeless.*) I'll make you sorry you made me want to marry you. (*At the hallway.*) I'll make you regret the day you ever decided to come to this college. I'll make you sorry you ever let yourself down. (*She exits. Silence. George sits still, staring straight ahead. Listening . . . but there is no sound. Outwardly calm, he returns to his book, reads a moment, then looks up . . . considers. . . .*)

GEORGE. "And the west, encumbered by crippling alliances, and burdened with a morality too rigid to accommodate itself to the swing of events, must . . . eventually . . . fall." (*He laughs, briefly, ruefully . . . rises, with the book in his hand. He stands still . . . then, quickly, he gathers all the fury he has been containing within himself . . . he shakes . . . he looks at the book in his hand and, with a cry that is part growl, part howl, he hurls it at the chimes. They crash against one another, ringing wildly. A brief pause, then Honey enters.*)

HONEY. (*The worse for wear, half asleep, still sick, weak, still staggering a little . . . vaguely, in something of a dream world.*) Bells. Ringing. I've been hearing bells.

GEORGE. Jesus!

HONEY. I couldn't sleep . . . for the bells. Ding-ding, bong . . . it woke me up. What time is it?

GEORGE. (*Quietly beside himself.*) Don't bother me.

HONEY. (*Confused and frightened.*) I was asleep, and the bells started . . . they BOOMED! Poe-bells . . . they were Poe-bells . . . Bing-bing-bong-BOOM!

GEORGE. BOOM!

HONEY. I was asleep, and I was dreaming of . . . something . . . and I heard the sounds coming, and I didn't know what it was.

GEORGE. (*Never quite to her.*) It was the sound of bodies. . . .

HONEY. And I didn't want to wake up, but the sound kept coming. . . .

GEORGE. . . . go back to sleep. . . .

HONEY. . . . and it FRIGHTENED ME!

GEORGE. (*Quietly . . . to Martha, as if she were in the room.*) I'm going to get you . . . Martha.

HONEY. And it was so . . . cold. The wind was . . . the wind was so cold! And I was lying somewhere, and the covers kept slipping away from me, and I didn't want them to. . . .

GEORGE. Somehow, Martha.

HONEY. . . . and there was someone there . . . !

GEORGE. There was no one there.

HONEY. (*Frightened.*) And I didn't want someone there . . . I was . . . naked . . . !

GEORGE. You don't know what's going on, do you?

HONEY. (*Still with her dream.*) I DON'T WANT ANY . . . NO . . . !

GEORGE. You don't know what's been going on around here while you been having your snoozette, do you?

HONEY. NO! . . . I DON'T WANT ANY . . . I DON'T WANT THEM. . . . GO 'WAY. . . . (*Begins to cry.*) I DON'T WANT . . ANY . . . CHILDREN. . . . I . . . don't . . . want . . . any . . . children. I'm afraid! I don't want to be hurt. . . . PLEASE!

GEORGE. (*Nodding his head . . . speaks with compassion.*) I should have known.

HONEY. (*Snapping awake from her reverie.*) What! What?

GEORGE. I should have known . . . the whole business . . . the headaches . . . the whining . . . the . . .

HONEY. (*Terrified.*) What are you talking about?

GEORGE. (*Ugly again.*) Does *he* know that? Does that . . . stud you're married to know about that, hunh?

HONEY. About what? Stay away from me!

GEORGE. Don't worry, baby . . . I wouldn't. . . . Oh, my God, that *would* be a joke, wouldn't it! But don't worry, baby. HEY! How you do it? Hunh? How do you make your secret little murders stud-boy doesn't know about, hunh? Pills? PILLS? You got a secret supply of pills? Or what? Apple jelly? WILL POWER?

HONEY. I feel sick.

GEORGE. You going to throw up again? You going to lie down

on the cold tiles, your knees pulled up under your chin, your thumb stuck in your mouth . . . ?

HONEY. (*Panicked.*) Where is he?

GEORGE. Where's who? There's nobody here, baby.

HONEY. I want my husband! I want a drink!

GEORGE. Well, you just crawl over to the bar and make yourself one. (*From off-stage comes the sound of Martha's laughter and the crashing of dishes. Yelling.*) That's right! Go at it!

HONEY. I want . . . something. . . .

GEORGE. You know what's going on in there, little Miss? Hunh? You hear all that? You know what's going on in there?

HONEY. I don't want to know anything!

GEORGE. There are a couple of people in there. . . . (*Martha's laughter again.*) . . . they are in there, in the kitchen. . . . Right there, with the onion skins and the coffee grounds . . . sort of . . . sort of a . . . sort of a dry run for the wave of the future.

HONEY. (*Beside herself.*) I . . . don't . . . understand . . . you. . . .

GEORGE. (*A hideous elation.*) It's very simple. . . . When people can't abide things as they are, when they can't abide the present, they do one of two things . . . either they . . . either they turn to a contemplation of the past, as I have done, or they set about to . . . alter the future. And when you want to change something . . . you BANG! BANG! BANG! BANG!

HONEY. Stop it!!

GEORGE. And you, you simpering bitch . . . you don't want children?

HONEY. You leave me . . . alone. Who . . . WHO RANG?

GEORGE. What?

HONEY. What were the bells? Who rang?

GEORGE. You don't want to know, do you? You don't want to listen to it, hunh?

HONEY. (*Shivering.*) I don't want to listen to you. . . . I want to know who rang.

GEORGE. Your husband is . . . and you want to know who rang?

HONEY. Who rang? Someone rang!

GEORGE. (*His jaw drops open. . . . He is whirling with an idea.*) . . . Someone . . .

HONEY. RANG!

GEORGE. . . . someone . . . rang . . . yes . . . yessss. . . .

HONEY. The . . . bells . . . rang. . . .

GEORGE. (*His mind racing ahead.*) The bells rang . . . and it was someone. . . .

HONEY. Somebody . . .

GEORGE. (*He is home, now.*) . . . somebody rang . . . it was somebody . . . with . . . I'VE GOT IT! I'VE GOT IT, MARTHA . . . ! Somebody with a message . . . and the message was . . . our son . . . OUR SON! (*Almost whispered.*) It was a message . . . the bells rang and it was a message, and it was about . . . our son . . . and the message . . . was . . . and the message was . . . our . . . son . . . is . . . DEAD!

HONEY. (*Almost sick.*) Oh . . . no.

GEORGE. (*Cementing it in his mind.*) Our son is . . . dead. . . . And . . . Martha doesn't know. . . . I haven't told . . . Martha.

HONEY. No . . . no . . . no.

GEORGE. (*Slowly, deliberately.*) Our son is dead, and Martha doesn't know.

HONEY. Oh. God in heaven . . . no.

GEORGE. (*To Honey . . . slowly, deliberately, dispassionately.*) And you're not going to tell her.

HONEY. (*In tears.*) Your son is dead.

GEORGE. I'll tell her myself . . . in good time. I'll tell her myself.

HONEY. (*So faintly.*) I'm going to be sick.

GEORGE. (*Turning away from her . . . he, too, softly.*) Are you? That's nice. (*Martha's laugh is heard again.*) Oh, listen to that.

HONEY. I'm going to die.

GEORGE. (*Quite by himself now.*) Good . . . good . . . you go right ahead. (*Very softly, so Martha could not possibly hear.*) Martha? Martha? I have some . . . terrible news for you. (*There is a strange half-smile on his lips.*) It's about our . . . son. He's dead. Can you hear me, Martha? Our boy is dead. (*He begins to laugh, very softly . . . it is mixed with crying.*)

CURTAIN

ACT THREE

THE EXORCISM

Martha enters, talking to herself.

MARTHA. Hey, hey. . . . Where is everybody . . . ? (*It is evident she is not bothered.*) So? Drop me; pluck me like a goddamn . . . whatever-it-is . . . creeping vine, and throw me over your shoulder like an old shoe . . . George? (*Looks about her.*) George? (*Silence.*) George! What are you doing: Hiding, or something? (*Silence.*) GEORGE!! (*Silence.*) Oh, fa Chri . . . (*Goes to the bar, makes herself a drink and amuses herself with the following performance.*) Deserted! Abandon-ed! Left out in the cold like an old pussy-cat. HA! Can I get you a drink, Martha? Why, thank you, George; that's very kind of you. No, Martha, no; why I'd do anything for you. Would you, George? Why, I'd do anything for you, too. Would you, Martha? Why, certainly, George. Martha, I've misjudged you. And I've misjudged you, too, George. WHERE IS EVERYBODY!!! Hump the Hostess! (*Laughs greatly at this, falls into a chair, calms down, looks defeated, says, softly.*) Fat chance. (*Even softer.*) Fat chance. (*Baby-talk now.*) Daddy? Daddy? Martha is abandon-ed. Left to her own vices at . . . (*Peers at a clock.*) . . . something o'clock in the old A.M. Daddy White-Mouse; do you really have red eyes? Do you? Let me see. Ohhhhh! You do! You do! Daddy, you have red eyes . . . because you cry all the time, don't you, Daddy. Yes; you do. You cry alllll the time. I'LL GIVE ALL YOU BASTARDS FIVE TO COME OUT FROM WHERE YOU'RE HIDING!! (*Pause.*) I cry all the time too, Daddy. I cry alllll the time; but deep inside, so no one can see me. I cry all he time. And Georgie cries all the time, too. We both cry all the time, and then, what we do, we cry, and we take our tears, and we put 'em in the ice box, in the goddamn ice trays (*Begins to laugh.*) until they're all frozen (*Laughs even more.*) and then . . . we put them . . . in our . . . drinks. (*More laughter, which is something else, too. After sobering silence.*) Up the drain, down the

86

spout, dead, gone and forgotten. . . . Up the spout, not down the spout; *Up* the spout: THE POKER NIGHT. Up the spout. . . . (*Sadly.*) I've got windshield wipers on my eyes, because I married you . . . baby! . . . Martha, you'll be a song-writer yet. (*Jiggles the ice in her glass.*) CLINK! (*Does it again.*) CLINK! (*Giggles, repeats it several times.*) CLINK! . . . CLINK! . . . CLINK! . . . CLINK! (*Nick enters while Martha is clinking; he stands in the hall entrance and watches her, finally he comes in.*)

NICK. My God, you've gone crazy too.

MARTHA. Clink?

NICK. I said, you've gone crazy too.

MARTHA. (*Considers it.*) Probably . . . probably.

NICK. You've all gone crazy: I come downstairs, and what happens. . . .

MARTHA. What happens?

NICK. . . . my wife's gone into the can with a liquor bottle, and she winks at me . . . winks at me! . . .

MARTHA. (*Sadly.*) She's never wunk at you; what a shame. . . .

NICK. She is lying down on the floor again, the tiles, all curled up, and she starts peeling the label off the liquor bottle, the brandy bottle. . . .

MARTHA. . . . we'll never get the deposit back that way. . . .

NICK. . . . and I ask her what she's doing, and she goes: shhhhhh!, nobody knows I'm here; and I come back in here, and you're sitting there going Clink!, for God's sake. Clink!

MARTHA. CLINK!

NICK. You've all gone crazy.

MARTHA. Yes. Sad but true.

NICK. Where is your husband?

MARTHA. He is vanish-ed. Pouf!

NICK. You're all crazy: nuts.

MARTHA. (*Affects a brogue.*) Awww, 'tis the refuge we take when the unreality of the world weighs too heavy on our tiny heads. (*Normal voice again.*) Relax; sink into it; you're no better than anybody else.

NICK. (*Wearily.*) I think I am.

MARTHA. (*Her glass to her mouth.*) You're certainly a flop in some departments.

NICK. (*Wincing.*) I beg your pardon . . . ?

MARTHA. (*Unnecessarily loud.*) I said, you're certainly a flop in some . . .

NICK. (*He, too, too loud.*) I'm sorry you're disappointed.

MARTHA. (*Braying.*) I didn't say I was disappointed! Stupid!

NICK. You should try me some time when we haven't been drinking for ten hours, and maybe . . .

MARTHA. (*Still braying.*) I wasn't talking about your potential; I was talking about your goddamn performance.

NICK. (*Softly.*) Oh.

MARTHA. (*She softer, too.*) Your potential's fine. It's dandy. (*Wiggles her eyebrows.*) Absolutely dandy. I haven't seen such a dandy potential in a long time. Oh, but baby, you sure are a flop.

NICK. (*Snapping it out.*) Everybody's a flop to you! Your husband's a flop, I'm a flop. . . .

MARTHA. (*Dismissing him.*) You're all flops. I am the Earth Mother, and you're all flops. (*More or less to herself.*) I disgust me. I pass my life in crummy, totally pointless infidelities . . . (*Laughs ruefully.*) would-be infidelities. Hump the Hostess? That's a laugh. A bunch of boozed-up . . . impotent lunk-heads. Martha makes goo-goo eyes, and the lunk-heads grin, and roll their beautiful, beautiful eyes back, and grin some more, and Martha licks her chops, and the lunk-heads slap over to the bar to pick up a little courage, *and* they pick up a little courage, and they bounce back over to old Martha, who does a little dance for them, which heats them all up . . . mentally . . . and so they slap over to the bar again, and pick up a little more courage, and their wives and sweethearts stick their noses up in the air . . . right through the ceiling, sometimes . . . which sends the lunk-heads back to the soda fountain again where they fuel up some more, while Martha-poo sits there with her dress up over her head . . . suffocating—you don't know how *stuffy* it is with your dress up over your head—suffocating! waiting for the lunk-heads; so, *finally* they get their courage up . . . but that's all, baby! Oh my, there is sometimes some very nice potential, but, oh my! My, my, my. (*Brightly.*) But that's how it is in a civilized society. (*To herself again.*) All the gorgeous lunk-heads. Poor babies. (*To Nick, now, earnestly.*) There is only one man in my life who has ever . . . made me happy. Do you know that? One!

88

NICK. The . . . the what-do-you-call-it? . . . uh . . . the lawn mower, or something?

MARTHA. No; I'd forgotten him. But when I think about him and me it's almost like being a voyeur. Hunh. No; I didn't mean him; I meant George, of course. (*No response from Nick.*) Uh . . . George; my husband.

NICK. (*Disbelieving.*) You're kidding.

MARTHA. Am I?

NICK. You must be. Him?

MARTHA. Him.

NICK. (*As if in on a joke.*) Sure; sure.

MARTHA. You don't believe it.

NICK. (*Mocking.*) Why, of course I do.

MARTHA. You always deal in appearances?

NICK. (*Derisively.*) Oh, for God's sake. . . .

MARTHA. . . . George who is out somewhere there in the dark. . . . George who is good to me, and whom I revile; who understands me, and whom I push off; who can make me laugh, and I choke it back in my throat; who can hold me, at night, so that it's warm, and whom I will bite so there's blood; who keeps learning the games we play as quickly as I can change the rules; who can make me happy and I do not wish to be happy, and yes I do wish to be happy. George and Martha: sad, sad, sad.

NICK. (*Echoing, still not believing.*) Sad.

MARTHA. . . . whom I will not forgive for having come to rest; for having seen me and having said: yes; this will do; who has made the hideous, the hurting, the insulting mistake of loving me and must be punished for it George and Martha: sad, sad, sad.

NICK. (*Puzzled.*) Sad.

MARTHA. . . . who tolerates, which is intolerable; who is kind, which is cruel; who understands, which is beyond comprehension. . . .

NICK. George and Martha: sad, sad, sad.

MARTHA. Some day . . . hah! some *night* . . . some stupid, liquor-ridden night . . . I will go too far . . . and I'll either break the man's back . . . or push him off for good . . . which is what I deserve.

NICK. I don't think he's got a vertebra intact.

MARTHA. (*Laughing at him.*) You don't, huh? You don't think so. Oh, little boy, you got yourself hunched over that microphone of yours. . . .

NICK. Microscope. . . .

MARTHA. . . . yes . . . and you don't see anything, do you? You see everything but the goddamn mind; you see all the little specs and crap, but you don't see what goes on, do you?

NICK. I know when a man's had his back broken; I can see that.

MARTHA. Can you!

NICK. You're damn right.

MARTHA. Oh . . . you know so little. And you're going to take over the world, hunh?

NICK. All right, now. . . .

MARTHA. You think a man's got his back broken 'cause he makes like a clown and walks bent, hunh? Is that *really* all you know?

NICK. I said, all *right!*

MARTHA. Ohhhh! The stallion's mad, hunh. The gelding's all upset. Ha, ha, ha, HA!

NICK. (*Softly; wounded.*) You . . . you swing wild, don't you.

MARTHA. (*Triumphant.*) HAH!

NICK. Just . . . anywhere.

MARTHA. HAH! I'm a gattling gun. Hahahahahahahahaha!

NICK. (*In wonder.*) Aimless . . . butchery. Pointless.

MARTHA. Aw! You poor little bastard.

NICK. Hit out at everything. (*The door chimes chime.*)

MARTHA. Go answer the door.

NICK. (*Amazed.*) What did you say?

MARTHA. I said, go answer the door. What are you, deaf?

NICK. (*Trying to get it straight.*) You . . . want me . . . to go answer the door?

MARTHA. That's right, lunk-head; answer the door. There must be something you can do well; or, are you too drunk to do that, too? Can't you get the latch up, either?

NICK. Look, there's no need . . . (*Door chimes again.*)

MARTHA. (*Shouting.*) Answer it! (*Softer.*) You can be house-boy around here for a while. You can start off being houseboy right now.

NICK. Look, lady, I'm no flunky to you.

MARTHA. (*Cheerfully.*) Sure you are! You're ambitious, aren't you, boy? You didn't chase me around the kitchen and up the

90

gaddamn stairs out of mad, driven passion, did you now? You were thinking a little bit about your career, weren't you? Well, you can just houseboy your way up the ladder for a while.

NICK. There's no limit to you, is there? (*Door chimes again.*)

MARTHA. (*Calmly, surely.*) No, baby; none. Go answer the door. (*Nick hesitates.*) Look, boy; once you stick your nose in it, you're not going to pull out just whenever you feel like it. You're in for a while. Now, git!

NICK. Aimless . . . wanton . . . pointless. . . .

MARTHA. Now, now, now; just do what you're told; show old Martha there's something you *can* do. Hunh? Atta boy.

NICK. (*Considers, gives in, moves toward the door. Chimes again.*) I'm coming, for Christ's sake!

MARTHA. (*Claps her hands.*) Ha HA! Wonderful; marvelous. (*Sings.*) "Just a gigolo, everywhere I go, people always say. . . ."

NICK. STOP THAT!

MARTHA. (*Giggles.*) Sorry, baby; go on now; open the little door.

NICK. (*With great rue.*) Christ. (*He flings open the door, and a hand thrusts into the opening a great bunch of snapdragons, they stay there for a moment. Nick strains his eyes to see who is behind them.*)

MARTHA. Oh, how lovely!

GEORGE. (*Appearing in the doorway, the snapdragons covering his face, speaks in a hideously cracked falsetto.*) Flores; flores para los muertos. Flores.

MARTHA. Ha, ha, ha HA!

GEORGE. (*A step into the room, lowers the flowers; sees Nick, his face becomes gleeful; he open his arms.*) Sonny! You've come home for your birthday! At last!

NICK. (*Backing off.*) Stay away from me.

MARTHA. Ha, ha, ha, HA! That's the houseboy, for God's sake.

GEORGE. Really? That's not our own little sonny-Jim? Our own little all-American something-or-other?

MARTHA. (*Giggling.*) Well, I certainly hope not; he's been acting awful funny, if he is.

GEORGE. (*Almost manic.*) Ohhhh! I'll bet! Chippie-chippie-chippie, hunh? (*Affecting embarrassment.*) I . . . I brungya dese flowers, Mart'a, 'cause I . . . well, 'cause you'se . . . awwwww hell. Gee.

MARTHA. Pansies! Rosemary! Violence! My wedding bouquet!

NICK. (*Starting to move away.*) Well, if you two kids don't mind, I think I'll just . . .

MARTHA. Ach! You just stay where you are. Make my hubby a drink.

NICK. I don't think I will.

GEORGE. No, Martha, no; that would be too much; he's your houseboy, baby, not mine.

NICK. I'm nobody's houseboy. . . .

GEORGE and MARTHA. . . . Now! (*Sing.*) I'm nobody's houseboy now. . . . (*Both laugh.*)

NICK. Vicious . . .

GEORGE. (*Finishing it for him.*) . . . children. Hunh? That right? Vicious children, with their oh-so-sad games, hopscotching their way through life, etcetera, etcetera. Is that it?

NICK. Something like it.

GEORGE. Screw, baby.

MARTHA. Him can't. Him too fulla booze.

GEORGE. Weally? (*Handing the snapdragons to Nick.*) Here; dump these in some gin. (*Nick takes them, looks at them, drops them on the floor at his feet.*)

MARTHA.. (*Sham dismay.*) Awwwwwww.

GEORGE. What a terrible thing to do . . . to Martha's snap-dragons.

MARTHA. Is that what they are?

GEORGE. Yup. And here I went out into the moonlight to pick 'em for Martha tonight, and for our sonny-boy tomorrow, for his birfday.

MARTHA. (*Passing on information.*) There is no moon now. I saw it go down from the bedroom.

GEORGE. (*Feigned glee.*) From the bedroom! (*Normal tone.*) Well, there was a moon.

MARTHA. (*Too patient, laughing a little.*) There couldn't have been a moon.

GEORGE. Well, there was. There is.

MARTHA. There is no moon; the moon went down.

GEORGE. There is a moon; the moon is up.

MARTHA. (*Straining to keep civil.*) I'm afraid you're mistaken.

GEORGE. (*Too cheerful.*) No; no.

MARTHA. (*Between her teeth.*) There is no goddamn moon.

GEORGE. My dear Martha . . . I did not pick snapdragons in the stony dark. I did not go stumbling around Daddy's greenhouse in the pitch.

MARTHA. Yes . . . you did. You would.

GEORGE. Martha, I do not pick flowers in the blink. I have never robbed a hothouse without there is a light from heaven.

MARTHA. (*With finality.*) There is no moon; the moon went down.

GEORGE. (*With great logic.*) That may very well be, Chastity; the moon may very well have gone down . . . but it came back up.

MARTHA. The moon does *not* come back up; when the moon has gone down it stays down.

GEORGE. (*Getting a little ugly.*) You don't know anything. IF the moon went down, then it came back up.

MARTHA. BULL!

GEORGE. Ignorance! Such . . . ignorance.

MARTHA. Watch who you're calling ignorant!

GEORGE. Once . . . once, when I was sailing past Majorca, drinking on deck with a correspondent who was talking about Roosevelt, the moon went down, thought about it for a little . . . considered it, you know what I mean? . . . and then, POP, came up again. Just like that.

MARTHA. That is not true! That is such a lie!

GEORGE. You must not call everything a lie, Martha. (*To Nick.*) Must she?

NICK. Hell, I don't know when you people are lying, or what

MARTHA You're damned right!

GEORGE. You're not supposed to.

MARTHA. Right!

GEORGE. At any rate, I was sailing past Majorca . . .

MARTHA. You never sailed past Majorca. . . .

GEORGE. Martha . . .

MARTHA. You were never in the goddamn Mediterranean at all . . . ever. . . .

GEORGE. I certainly was! My Mommy and Daddy took me there as a college graduation present.

MARTHA. Nuts!

NICK. Was this after you killed them? (*George and Martha swing around and look at him; there is a brief, ugly pause.*)

GEORGE. (*Defiantly.*) Maybe.

MARTHA. Yeah; maybe not, too.

NICK. Jesus! (*George swoops down, picks up the bunch of snapdragons, shakes them like a feather duster in Nick's face, and moves away a little.*)

GEORGE. HAH!

NICK. Damn you.

GEORGE. (*To Nick.*) Truth and illusion. Who knows the difference, eh, toots? Eh?

MARTHA. You were never in the Mediterranean . . . truth or illusion . . . either way.

GEORGE. If I wasn't in the Mediterranean, how did I get to the Aegean? Hunh?

MARTHA. OVERLAND!

NICK. Yeah!

GEORGE. Don't you side with her, houseboy.

NICK. I am not a houseboy.

GEORGE. Look! I know the game! You don't make it in the sack, you're a houseboy.

NICK. I AM NOT A HOUSEBOY!

GEORGE. No? Well then, you must have made it in the sack. Yes? (*He is breathing a little heavy; behaving a little manic.*) Yes? Someone's lying around here; somebody isn't playing the game straight. Yes? Come on; come on; who's lying? Martha? Come on!

NICK. (*After a pause; to Martha, quietly with intense pleading.*) Tell him I'm not a houseboy.

MARTHA. (*After a pause, quietly, lowering her head.*) No; you're not a houseboy.

GEORGE. (*With great, sad relief.*) So be it.

MARTHA. (*Pleading.*) Truth and illusion, George; you don't know the difference.

GEORGE. No; but we must carry on as though we did.

MARTHA. Amen.

GEORGE. (*Flourishing the flowers.*) SNAP WENT THE DRAGONS!! (*Nick and Martha laugh weakly.*) Hunh? Here we go round the mulberry bush, Hunh?

NICK. (*Tenderly, to Martha.*) Thank you.

MARTHA. Skip it.

GEORGE. (*Loud.*) I said, here we go round the mulberry bush!

MARTHA. (*Impatiently.*) Yeah, yeah; we know; snap go the dragons.

GEORGE. (*Taking a snapdragon, throwing it, spear-like, stem first at Martha.*) SNAP!

MARTHA. Don't, George.

GEORGE. (*Throws another.*) SNAP!

NICK. Don't do that.

GEORGE. Shut up, stud.

NICK. I'm not a stud!

GEORGE. (*Throws one at Nick.*) SNAP! Then you're a houseboy. Which is it? Which are you? Hunh? Make up your mind. Either way. . . . (*Throws another at him.*) SNAP! . . . *you disgust me.*

MARTHA. Does it matter to you, George?

GEORGE. (*Throws one at her.*) SNAP! No, actually, it doesn't. Either way . . . I've had it.

MARTHA. Stop throwing those goddamn things at me!

GEORGE. Either way. (*Throws another at her.*) SNAP!

NICK. (*To Martha.*) Do you want me to . . . do something to him?

MARTHA. You leave him alone!

GEORGE. If you're a houseboy, baby, you can pick up after me; if you're a stud, you can go protect your plow. Either way. Either way. . . . Everything.

NICK. Oh for God's . . .

MARTHA. (*A little afraid.*) Truth or illusion, George. Doesn't it matter to you . . . at all?

GEORGE. (*Without throwing anything.*) SNAP! (*Silence.*) You got your answer, baby?

MARTHA. (*Sadly.*) Got it.

GEORGE. You just gird your blue-veined loins, girl. (*Sees Nick moving toward the hall.*) Now; we got one more game to play. And it's called Bringing Up Baby.

NICK. (*More-or-less under his breath.*) Oh, for Lord's sake. . . .

MARTHA. George . . .

GEORGE. I don't want any fuss. (*To Nick.*) You don't want any scandal around here, do you, big boy? You don't want to wreck things, do you? Hunh? You want to keep to your time table, don't you? Then sit! (*Nick sits. To Martha.*) And you, pretty Miss, you like fun and games, don't you? You're a sport from way back, aren't you?

MARTHA. (*Quietly, giving in.*) All right, George; all right.

GEORGE. (*Seeing them both cowed, purrs.*) Gooooooooood; gooooood. (*Looks about him.*) But, we're not all here. (*Snaps his fingers a couple of times at Nick.*) You; you . . . uh . . . you; your little wifelet isn't here.

NICK. Look; she's had a rough night, now; she's in the can, and she's . . .

GEORGE. Well, we can't play without everyone here. Now that's a fact. We gotta have your little wife. (*Hog-calls toward the hall.*) SOOOWWWIIIEEE!! SOOOWWWIIIEEE!!

NICK. (*As Martha giggles nervously.*) Cut that!

GEORGE. (*Swinging around, facing him.*) Then get your butt out of that chair and bring the little dip back in here. (*As Nick does not move.*) Now be a good puppy. Fetch, good puppy, go fetch. (*Nick rises, opens his mouth to say something, thinks better of it, exits.*) One more game.

MARTHA. (*After Nick goes.*) I don't like what's going to happen.

GEORGE. (*Surprisingly tender.*) Do you know what it is?

MARTHA. (*Pathetic.*) No. But I don't like it.

GEORGE. Maybe you will, Martha.

MARTHA. No.

GEORGE. Oh, it's a real fun game, Martha.

MARTHA. (*Pleading.*) No more games.

GEORGE. (*Quietly triumphant.*) One more, Martha. One more game, and then beddie-bye. Everybody pack up his tools and baggage and stuff and go home. And you and me, well, we gonna climb them well worn stairs.

MARTHA. (*Almost in tears.*) No, George; no.

GEORGE. (*Soothing.*) Yes, baby.

MARTHA. No, George; please?

GEORGE. It'll all be done with before you know it.

MARTHA. No, George.

GEORGE. No climb stairs with Georgie?

MARTHA. (*A sleepy child.*) No more games . . . please. It's games I don't want. No more games.

GEORGE. Aw, sure you do, Martha . . . original game-girl and all, 'course you do.

MARTHA. Ugly games . . . ugly. And now this new one?

GEORGE. (*Stroking her hair.*) You'll love it, baby.

MARTHA. No, George.

GEORGE. You'll have a ball.

MARTHA. (*Tenderly; moves to touch him.*) Please, George, no more games; I . . .

GEORGE. (*Slapping her moving hand with vehemence.*) Don't you touch me! You keep your paws clean for the undergraduates!

MARTHA. (*A cry of alarm, but faint.*)

GEORGE. (*Grabbing her hair, pulling her head back.*) Now, you listen to me, Martha; you have had quite an evening . . . quite a night for yourself, and you can't just cut it off whenever you've got enough blood in your mouth. We are going on, and I'm going to have at you, and it's going to make your performance tonight look like an Easter pageant. Now I want you to get yourself a little alert. (*Slaps her lightly with his free hand.*) I want a little life in you, baby. (*Again.*)

MARTHA. (*Struggling.*) Stop it!

GEORGE. (*Again.*) Pull yourself together! (*Again.*) I want you on your feet and slugging, sweetheart, because I'm going to knock you around, and I want you up for it. (*Again, he pulls away, releases her; she rises.*)

MARTHA. All right, George. What do you want, George?

GEORGE. An equal battle, baby; that's all.

MARTHA. You'll get it!

GEORGE. I want you mad.

MARTHA. I'M MAD!!

GEORGE. Get madder!

MARTHA. DON'T WORRY ABOUT IT!

GEORGE. Good for you, girl; now, we're going to play this one to the death.

MARTHA. Yours!

GEORGE. You'd be surprised. Now, here come the tots; you be ready for this.

MARTHA. (*She paces, actually looks a bit like a fighter.*) I'm ready for you. (*Nick and Honey re-enter; Nick supporting Honey, who still retains her brandy bottle and glass.*)

NICK. (*Unhappily.*) Here we are.

HONEY. (*Cheerfully.*) Hip, hop. Hip, hop.

NICK. You a bunny, Honey? (*She laughs greatly, sits.*)

HONEY. I'm a bunny, Honey.

GEORGE. (*To Honey.*) Well, now; how's the bunny?

HONEY. Bunny funny! (*She laughs again.*)

NICK. (*Under his breath.*) Jesus.

GEORGE. Bunny funny? Good for bunny!

MARTHA. Come on, George!

GEORGE. (*To Martha.*) Honey funny bunny! (*Honey screams with laughter.*)

NICK. Jesus God . . .

GEORGE. (*Slaps his hands together, once.*) All right! Here we go! Last game! All sit. (*Nick sits.*) Sit down, Martha. This is a civilized game.

MARTHA. (*Cocks her fist, doesn't swing. Sits.*) Just get on with it.

HONEY. (*To George.*) I've decided I don't remember anything. (*To Nick.*) Hello, Dear.

GEORGE. Hunh? What?

MARTHA. It's almost dawn, for God's sake. . . .

HONEY. (*Ibid.*) I don't remember anything, and you don't remember anything, either. Hello, Dear.

GEORGE. You what?

HONEY. (*Ibid. An edge creeping into her voice.*) You heard me, nothing. Hello, Dear.

GEORGE. (*To Honey, referring to Nick.*) You do know that's your husband, there, don't you?

HONEY. (*With great dignity.*) Well, I certainly know *that.*

GEORGE. (*Close to Honey's ear.*) It's just some things you can't remember . . . hunh?

HONEY. (*A great laugh to cover; then quietly, intensely to George.*) Don't remember; not can't. (*At Nick, cheerfully.*) Hello, Dear.

GEORGE. (*To Nick.*) Well, speak to your little wifelet, your little bunny, for God's sake.

NICK. (*Softly, embarrassed.*) Hello, Honey.

GEORGE. Awww, that was nice. I think we've been having a . . . a real good evening . . . all things considered. . . . We've sat around, and got to know each other, and had fun and games . . . curl-up-on-the-floor, for example. . . .

HONEY. . . . the tiles. . . .

GEORGE. . . . the tiles. . . . Snap the Dragon.

98

HONEY. . . . peel the label. . . .

GEORGE. . . . peel the . . . what?

MARTHA. Label. Peel the label.

HONEY. (*Apologetically, holding up her brandy bottle.*) I peel labels.

GEORGE. We all peel labels, sweetie; and when you get through the skin, all three layers, through the muscle, slosh aside the organs (*An aside to Nick.*) them which is still sloshable—(*Back to Honey.*) and get down to bone . . . you know what you do then?

HONEY. (*Terribly interested.*) No!

GEORGE. When you get down to bone, you haven't got all the way, yet. There's something inside the bone . . . the marrow . . . and that's what you gotta get at. (*A strange smile at Martha.*)

HONEY. Oh! I see.

GEORGE. The marrow. But bones are pretty resilient, especially in the young. Now, take our son. . . .

HONEY. (*Strangely.*) Who?

GEORGE. Our son. . . . Martha's and my little joy!

NICK. (*Moving toward the bar.*) Do you mind if I . . . ?

GEORGE. No, no, you go right ahead.

MARTHA. George . . .

GEORGE. (*Too kindly.*) Yes, Martha?

MARTHA. Just what are you doing?

GEORGE. Why, love, I was talking about our son.

MARTHA. Don't.

GEORGE. Isn't Martha something? Here we are, on the eve of our boy's home-coming, the eve of the twenty-first birfday, the eve of his majority . . . and Martha says don't talk about him.

MARTHA. Just . . . don't.

GEORGE. But I want to, Martha! It's very important we talk about him. Now bunny and the . . . well, whichever he is . . . here don't know much about junior, and I think they should.

MARTHA. Just . . . don't.

GEORGE. (*Snapping his fingers at Nick.*) You. Hey, you! You want to play Bringing Up Baby, don't you!

NICK. (*Hardly civil.*) Were you snapping at me?

GEORGE. That's right. (*Instructing him.*) *You* want to hear about our bouncy boy.

NICK. (*Pause, then, shortly.*) Yeah; sure.

GEORGE. (*To Honey.*) And you, my dear? You want to hear about him, too, don't you.

HONEY. (*Pretending not to understand.*) Whom?

GEORGE. Martha's and my son.

HONEY. (*Nervously.*) Oh, you have a child? (*Martha and Nick laugh uncomfortably.*)

GEORGE. Oh, indeed; do we ever! Do you want to talk about him, Martha, or shall I? Hunh?

MARTHA. (*A smile that is a sneer.*) Don't, George.

GEORGE. All rightie. Well, now; let's see. He's a nice kid, really, in spite of his home life; I mean most kids'd grow up neurotic, what with Martha here carrying on the way she does: sleeping till four in the P.M., climbing all over the poor bastard, trying to break the bathroom door down to wash him in the tub when he's sixteen, dragging strangers into the house at all hours. . . .

MARTHA. (*Rising.*) O.K. YOU!

GEORGE. (*Mock concern.*) Martha!

MARTHA. That's enough!

GEORGE. Well, do you want to take over?

HONEY. (*To Nick.*) Why would anybody want to wash somebody who's sixteen years old?

NICK. (*Slamming his drink down.*) Oh, for Christ's sake, Honey!

HONEY. (*Stage whisper.*) Well, why?!

GEORGE. Because it's her baby-poo.

MARTHA. ALL RIGHT!! (*By rote, a kind of almost-tearful recitation.*) Our son. You want our son? You'll have it.

GEORGE. You want a drink, Martha?

MARTHA. (*Pathetically.*) Yes.

NICK. (*To Martha kindly.*) We don't have to hear about it . . . if you don't want to.

GEORGE. Who says so? You in a position to set the rules around here?

NICK. (*Pause; tight-lipped.*) No.

GEORGE. Good boy; you'll go far. All right, Martha; your recitation, please.

MARTHA. (*From far away.*) What, George?

GEORGE. (*Prompting.*) "Our son . . ."

MARTHA. All right. Our son. Our son was born in a September

night, a night not unlike tonight, though tomorrow, and twenty . . . one . . . years ago.

GEORGE. (*Beginning of quiet asides.*) You see? I told you.

MARTHA. It was an easy birth. . . .

GEORGE. Oh, Martha; no. You labored . . . how you labored.

MARTHA. It was an easy birth . . . once it had been . . . accepted, relaxed into.

GEORGE. Ah . . . yes. Better.

MARTHA. It was an easy birth, once it had been accepted, and I was young.

GEORGE. And I was younger. . . . (*Laughs quietly to himself.*)

MARTHA. And I was young, and he was a healthy child, a red, bawling child, with slippery firm limbs. . . .

GEORGE. . . . Martha thinks she saw him at delivery. . . .

MARTHA. . . . with slippery, firm limbs, and a full head of black, fine, fine hair which, oh, later, later, became blond as the sun, our son.

GEORGE. He was a healthy child.

MARTHA. And I had wanted a child . . . oh, I had wanted a child.

GEORGE. (*Prodding her.*) A son? A daughter?

MARTHA. A child! (*Quieter.*) A child. And I had my child.

GEORGE. Our child.

MARTHA. (*With great sadness.*) Our child. And we raised him . . . (*Laughs, briefly, bitterly.*) yes, we did; we raised him. . . .

GEORGE. With teddy bears and an antique bassinet from Austria . . . and no murav.

MARTHA. . . . with teddy bears and transparent floating goldfish, and a pale blue bed with cane at the headboard when he was older, cane which he wore through . . . finally . . . with his little hands . . . in his . . . sleep. . . .

GEORGE. . . . nightmares. . . .

MARTHA. . . . *sleep.* . . . He was a restless child. . . .

GEORGE. . . . (*Soft chuckle, head-shaking of disbelief.*) . . . Oh Lord . . .

MARTHA. . . . sleep . . . and a croup tent . . . a pale green croup tent, and the shining kettle hissing in the one light of the room that time he was sick . . . those four days . . . and animal crackers, and the bow and arrow he kept under his bed. . . .

101

GEORGE. . . . the arrows with rubber cups at their tip. . . .

MARTHA. . . . at their tip, which he kept beneath his bed. . . .

GEORGE. Why? Why, Martha?

MARTHA. . . . for fear . . . for fear of . . .

GEORGE. For fear. Just that: for fear.

MARTHA. (*Vaguely waving him off, going on.*) . . . and . . . and sandwiches on Sunday night, and Saturdays . . . (*Pleased recollection.*) . . . and Saturdays the banana boat, the whole peeled banana, scooped out on top, with green grapes for the crew, a double line of green grapes, and along the sides, stuck to the boat with toothpicks, orange slices. . . . SHIELDS.

GEORGE. And for the oar?

MARTHA. (*Uncertainly.*) A . . . carrot?

GEORGE. Or a swizzle stick, whatever was easier.

MARTHA. No. A carrot. And his eyes were green . . . green with . . . if you peered so deep into them . . . so deep . . . bronze . . . bronze parentheses around the irises . . . such green eyes!

GEORGE. . . . blue, green, brown . . .

MARTHA. . . . and he loved the sun! . . . He was tan before and after everyone . . . and in the sun his hair . . . became . . . fleece.

GEORGE. (*Echoing her.*) . . . fleece . . .

MARTHA. . . . beautiful, beautiful boy.

GEORGE. Absolve, Domine, animas omnium fidelium defunctorum ab omni vinculo delictorum.

MARTHA. . . . and school . . . and summer camp . . . and sledding . . . and swimming. . . .

GEORGE. Et gratia tua illis succurrente, mereantur evadere judicium ultionis.

MARTHA. (*Laughing, to herself.*) . . . and how he broke his arm . . . how funny it was . . . oh, no, it hurt him! . . . but, oh, it was funny . . . in a field, his very first cow, the first he'd ever seen . . . and he went into the field, to the cow, where the cow was grazing, head down, busy . . . and he moo'd at it! (*Laughs ibid.*) He moo'd at it . . . and the beast, oh, surprised, swung its head up and moo'd at him, all three years of him, and he ran, startled, and he stumbled . . . fell . . . and broke his poor arm. (*Laughs, ibid.*) Poor lamb.

GEORGE. Et lucis aeternae beatitudine perfrui.

102

MARTHA. George cried! Helpless . . . George . . . cried. I carried the poor lamb. George snuffling beside me, I carried the child, having fashioned a sling . . . and across the great fields.

GEORGE. In Paradisum deducant te Angeli.

MARTHA. And as he grew . . . and as he grew . . . oh! so wise! . . . he walked evenly between us . . . (*She spreads her hands,*) . . . a hand out to each of us for what we could offer by way of support, affection, teaching, even love . . . and these hands, still, to hold us off a bit, for mutual protection, to protect us all from George's . . . weakness . . . and my . . . necessary greater strength . . . to protect himself . . . and *us.*

GEORGE. In memoria aeterna erit justus: ab auditione mala non timebit.

MARTHA. So wise, so wise.

NICK. (*To George.*) What is this? What are you doing?

GEORGE. Shhhhh.

HONEY. Shhhhh.

NICK. (*Shrugging.*) O.K.

MARTHA. So beautiful; so wise.

GEORGE. (*Laughs quietly.*) All truth being relative.

MARTHA. It was true! Beautiful; wise; perfect.

GEORGE. There's a real mother talking.

HONEY. (*Suddenly, almost tearfully.*) I want a child.

NICK. Honey . . .

HONEY. (*More forcefully.*) I want a child!

GEORGE. On principle?

HONEY. (*In tears.*) I want a child, I want a baby.

MARTHA. (*Waiting out the interruption, not really paying it any mind.*) Of course, this state, this perfection . . . couldn't last. Not with George . . . not with George around.

GEORGE. (*To the others.*) There; you see? I knew she'd shift.

HONEY. Be still!

GEORGE. (*Mock awe.*) Sorry . . . mother.

NICK. Can't you be still?

GEORGE. (*Making a sign at Nick.*) Dominus vobiscum.

MARTHA. Not with George around. A drowning man takes down those nearest. George tried, but, oh, God, how I fought him. God, how I fought him.

GEORGE. (*A satisfied laugh.*) Ahhhhhhh.

MARTHA. Lesser states can't stand those above them. Weakness,

103

imperfection cries out against strength, goodness and innocence. And George tried.

GEORGE. How did I try, Martha? How did I try?

MARTHA. How did you . . . what? . . . No! No . . . he grew . . . our son grew . . . up; he is grown up; he is away at school, college. He is fine, everything is fine.

GEORGE. (*Mocking.*) Oh, come on, Martha!

MARTHA. No. That's all.

GEORGE. Just a minute! You can't cut a story off like that, sweetheart. You started to say something . . . now you say it!

MARTHA. No!

GEORGE. Well, I will.

MARTHA. No!

GEORGE. You see, Martha, here, stops just when the going gets good . . . just when things start getting a little rough. Now, Martha, here, is a misunderstood little girl; she really is. Not only does she have a husband who is a bog . . . a younger-than-she-is bog albeit . . . not only does she have a husband who is a bog, she has as well a tiny problem with spiritous liquors—like she can't get enough. . . .

MARTHA. (*Without energy.*) No more, George.

GEORGE. . . . and on top of all that, poor weighed-down girl, PLUS a father who really doesn't give a damn whether she lives or dies, who couldn't care less *what* happens to his only daughter . . . on top of all that she has a *son*. She has a son who fought her every inch of the way, who didn't want to be turned into a weapon against his father, who didn't want to be used as a goddamn club whenever Martha didn't get things l e she wanted them!

MARTHA. (*Rising to it.*) Lies! Lies!!

GEORGE. Lies? All right. A son who would *not* disown his father, who came to him for advice, for information, for love that wasn't mixed with sickness—and you know what I mean, Martha!—who could not tolerate the slashing, braying residue that called itself his MOTHER. MOTHER? HAH!!

MARTHA. (*Cold.*) All right, you. A son who was so ashamed of his father he asked me once if it—possibly—wasn't true, as he had heard, from some cruel boys, maybe, that he was not our child; who could not tolerate the shabby failure his father had become. . . .

104

GEORGE. Lies!

MARTHA. Lies? Who would not bring his girl friends to the house . . .

GEORGE. . . . in shame of his mother. . . .

MARTHA. . . . of his father! Who writes letters only to me!

GEORGE. Oh, so you think! To me! At my office!

MARTHA. Liar!

GEORGE. I have a stack of them.

MARTHA. YOU HAVE NO LETTERS!

GEORGE. And you have?

MARTHA. He has no letters. A son . . . a son who spends his summers away . . . away from his family . . . ON ANY PRETEXT . . . because he can't stand the shadow of a man flickering around the edges of a house. . . .

GEORGE. . . . who spends his summers away . . . and he does! . . . who spends his summers away because there isn't room for him in a house full of empty bottles, lies, strange men, and a harridan who . . .

MARTHA. Liar!!

GEORGE. Liar?

MARTHA. . . . A son who I have raised as best I can against . . . vicious odds, against the corruption of weakness and petty revenges. . . .

GEORGE. . . . A son who is, deep in his gut, sorry to have been born. . . . (*Both together.*)

MARTHA. I have tried, oh God, I have tried; the one thing . . . the one thing I've tried to carry pure and unscathed through the sewer of this marriage; through the sick nights, and the pathetic, stupid days, through the derision and the laughter . . . *God,* the laughter, through one failure after another, one failure compounding another failure, each attempt more sickening, more numbing than the one before; the one thing, the one *person*

GEORGE. Libera me, Domine, de morte aeterna, in die illa tremenda: Quando caeli movendi sunt et terra: Dum veneris judicare saeculum per ignem. Tremens factus sum ego, et timeo, dum discussio venerit, atque ventura ira. Quando caeli movendi sunt et terra. Dies illa, dies irae, calamitatis et miseriae; dies magna et amara valde. Dum veneris judicare saeculum per ignem. Requiem aeternam dona eis, Domine: et lux perpetua

105

I have tried to protect, to raise above the mire of this vile, crushing marriage; the one light in all this hopeless . . . *dark*ness . . . our SON.

luceat eis. Libera me Domine de morte aeterna in die illa tremenda: quando caeli movendi sunt et terra; Dum veneris judicare saeculum per ignem.

(*End together.*)

HONEY. (*Her hands to her ears.*) STOP IT!! STOP IT!!

GEORGE. (*With a hand sign.*) Kyrie, eleison. Christe, eleison. Kyrie, eleison.

HONEY. JUST STOP IT!!

GEORGE. Why, baby? Don't you like it?

HONEY. (*Quite hysterical.*) You . . . can't . . . do . . . this!

GEORGE. (*Triumphant.*) Who says!

HONEY. I! Say!

GEORGE. Tell us why, baby.

HONEY. No!

NICK. Is this game over?

HONEY. Yes! Yes, it is.

GEORGE. Ho-ho! Not by a long shot. (*To Martha.*) We got a little surprise for you, baby. It's about sunny-Jim.

MARTHA. No more, George.

GEORGE. YES!

NICK. Leave her be!

GEORGE. I'M RUNNING THIS SHOW! (*To Martha.*) Sweetheart, I'm afraid I've got some bad news for you . . . for us, of course. Some rather sad news. (*Honey begins weeping, head in hands.*)

MARTHA. (*Afraid, suspicious.*) What is this?

GEORGE. (*Oh, so patiently.*) Well, Martha, while you were out of the room, while the . . . two of you were out of the room . . . I mean, I don't know where, hell, you both must have been somewhere. (*Little laugh.*) . . . While you were out of the room, for a while . . . well, Missey and I were sittin' here havin' a little talk, you know: a chaw and a talk . . . and the doorbell rang. . . .

HONEY. (*Head still in hands.*) Chimed.

GEORGE. Chimed . . . and . . . well, it's hard to tell you, Martha. . . .

MARTHA. (*A strange throaty voice.*) Tell me.

HONEY. Please . . . don't.

MARTHA. Tell me.

GEORGE. . . . and . . . what it was . . . it was good old Western Union, some little boy about seventy.

MARTHA. (Involved.) Crazy Billy?

GEORGE. Yes, Martha, that's right . . . crazy Billy . . . and he had a telegram, and it was for us, and I have to tell you about it.

MARTHA. (As if from a distance.) Why didn't they phone it? Why did they bring it; why didn't they telephone it?

GEORGE. Some telegrams you have to deliver, Martha; some telegrams you can't phone.

MARTHA. (Rising.) What do you mean?

GEORGE. Martha. . . . I can hardly bring myself to say it. . . .

HONEY. Don't.

GEORGE. (To Honey.) Do you want to do it?

HONEY. (Defending herself against an attack of bees.) No no no no no.

GEORGE. (Sighing heavily.) All right. Well, Martha . . . I'm afraid our boy isn't coming home for his birthday.

MARTHA. Of course he is.

GEORGE. No, Martha.

MARTHA. Of course he is. I say he is!

GEORGE. He . . . can't.

MARTHA. He is! I say so!

GEORGE. Martha . . . (Long pause.) . . . our son is . . . dead. (Silence.) He was . . . killed . . . late in the afternoon . . . (Silence. A tiny chuckle.) on a country road, with his learner's permit in his pocket, he swerved, to avoid a porcupine, and drove straight into a . . .

MARTHA. (Rigid fury.) YOU . . . CAN'T . . . DO . . . THAT!

GEORGE. . . . large tree.

MARTHA. YOU CANNOT DO THAT!

NICK. (Softly.) Oh my God. (Honey is weeping louder.)

GEORGE. (Quietly, dispassionately.) I thought you should know.

NICK. Oh my God; no.

MARTHA. (Quivering with rage and loss.) NO! NO! YOU CANNOT DO THAT! YOU CAN'T DECIDE THAT FOR YOURSELF! I WILL NOT LET YOU DO THAT!

GEORGE. We'll have to leave around noon, I suppose. . . .

MARTHA. I WILL NOT LET YOU DECIDE THESE THINGS!

107

GEORGE. . . . because there are matters of identification, naturally, and arrangements to be made. . . .

MARTHA. (*Leaping at George, but ineffectual.*) YOU CAN'T DO THIS! (*Nick rises, grabs hold of Martha, pins her arms behind her back.*) I WON'T LET YOU DO THIS, GET YOUR HANDS OFF ME!

GEORGE. (*As Nick holds on, right in Martha's face.*) You don't seem to understand, Martha; I haven't done anything. Now, pull yourself together. Our son is DEAD! Can you get that into your head?

MARTHA. YOU CAN'T DECIDE THESE THINGS.

NICK. Lady, please.

MARTHA. LET ME GO!

GEORGE. Now listen, Martha; listen carefully. We got a telegram; there was a car accident, and he's dead. POUF! Just like that! Now, how do you like it?

MARTHA. (*A howl which weakens into a moan.*) NOOOOOO-oooooo.

GEORGE. (*To Nick.*) Let her go. (*Martha slumps to the floor in a sitting position.*) She'll be all right now.

MARTHA. (*Pathetic.*) No; no, he is *not* dead; he is not *dead.*

GEORGE. He is dead. Kyrie, eleison. Christe, eleison. Kyrie, eleison.

MARTHA. You cannot. You may not decide these things.

NICK. (*Leaning over her, tenderly.*) He hasn't decided anything, lady. It's not his doing. He doesn't have the power. . . .

GEORGE. That's right, Martha; I'm not a God. I don't have the power over life and death, do I?

MARTHA. YOU CAN'T KILL HIM! YOU CAN'T HAVE HIM DIE!

HONEY. Lady . . . please . . .

MARTHA. YOU CAN'T!

GEORGE. There was a telegram, Martha.

MARTHA. (*Up, facing him.*) Show it to me! Show me the telegram!

GEORGE. (*Long pause, then, with a straight face.*) I ate it.

MARTHA. (*A pause, then with the greatest disbelief possible, tinged with hysteria.*) What did you just say to me?

GEORGE. (*Barely able to stop exploding with laughter.*) I . . . ate . . . it. (*Martha stares at him for a long moment, then spits in his face. George, with a smile.*) Good for you, Martha.

108

NICK. (*To George.*) Do you think that's the way to treat her at a time like this? Making an ugly goddamn joke like that? Hunh?

GEORGE. (*Snapping his fingers at Honey.*) Did I eat the telegram or did I not?

HONEY. (*Terrified.*) Yes; yes, you ate it. I watched . . . I watched you . . . you . . . you ate it all down.

GEORGE. (*Prompting.*) . . . like a good boy.

HONEY. . . . like a . . . g-g-g-good . . . boy. Yes.

MARTHA (*To George, coldly.*) You're not going to get away with this.

GEORGE. (*With disgust.*) YOU KNOW THE RULES, MARTHA! FOR CHRIST'S SAKE, YOU KNOW THE RULES!

MARTHA. NO!

NICK. (*With the beginning of a knowledge he cannot face.*) What are you two talking about?

GEORGE. I can kill him, Martha, if I want to.

MARTHA. HE IS OUR CHILD!

GEORGE. Oh yes, and you bore him, and it was a good delivery. . . .

MARTHA. HE IS OUR CHILD!

GEORGE. AND I HAVE KILLED HIM!

MARTHA. NO!

GEORGE. YES! (*Long silence.*)

NICK. (*Very quietly.*) I think I understand this.

GEORGE. (*Ibid.*) Do you?

NICK. (*Ibid.*) Jesus Christ, I think I understand this.

GEORGE. (*Ibid.*) Good for you, buster.

NICK. (*Violently.*) JESUS CHRIST I THINK I UNDERSTAND THIS!

MARTHA. (*Great sadness and loss.*) You have no right . . . you have no right at all . . .

GEORGE. (*Tenderly.*) I have the right, Martha. We never spoke of it; that's all. I could kill him any time I wanted to.

MARTHA. But why? Why?

GEORGE. You broke our rule, baby. You mentioned him . . . you mentioned him to someone else.

MARTHA. (*Tearfully.*) I did not. I never did.

GEORGE. Yes, you did.

MARTHA. Who? WHO?!

HONEY. (*Crying.*) To me. You mentioned him to me.

MARTHA. (*Crying.*) I FORGET! Sometimes . . . sometimes when

it's night, when it's late, and . . . and everybody else is . . .
talking . . . I forget and I . . . want to mention him . . . but
I . . . HOLD ON . . . I hold on . . . but I've wanted to . . .
so often . . . oh, George, you've *pushed* it . . . there was no
need . . . there was no need for *this*. I *mentioned* him . . . all
right . . . but you didn't have to push it over the EDGE. You
didn't have to . . . kill him.

GEORGE. Requiescat in pace.

HONEY. Amen.

MARTHA. You didn't have to have him die, George.

GEORGE. Requiem aeternam dona eis, Domine.

HONEY. Et lux perpetua luceat eis.

MARTHA. That wasn't . . . needed. (*A long silence.*)

GEORGE. (*Softly.*) It will be dawn soon. I think the party's
over.

NICK. (*To George, quietly.*) You couldn't have . . . any?

GEORGE. *We* couldn't.

MARTHA. (*A hint of communion in this.*) *We* couldn't.

GEORGE. (*To Nick and Honey.*) Home to bed, children; it's way
past your bedtime.

NICK. (*His hand out to Honey.*) Honey?

HONEY. (*Rising, moving to him.*) Yes.

GEORGE. (*Martha is sitting on the floor by a chair now.*) You
two go now.

NICK. Yes.

HONEY. Yes.

NICK. I'd like to. . . .

GEORGE. Good night.

NICK. (*Pause.*) Good night. (*Nick and Honey exit, George
closes the door after them, looks around the room, sighs, picks up
a glass or two, takes it to the bar. This whole last section very
softly, very slowly.*)

GEORGE. Do you want anything, Martha?

MARTHA. (*Still looking away.*) No . . . nothing.

GEORGE. All right. (*Pause.*) Time for bed.

MARTHA. Yes.

GEORGE. Are you tired?

MARTHA. Yes.

GEORGE. I am.

MARTHA. Yes.

GEORGE. Sunday tomorrow; all day.

MARTHA. Yes. (*A long silence between them.*) Did you . . . did you . . . have to?

GEORGE. (*Pause.*) Yes.

MARTHA. It was . . . ? You had to?

GEORGE. (*Pause.*) Yes.

MARTHA. I don't know.

GEORGE. It was . . . time.

MARTHA. Was it?

GEORGE. Yes.

MARTHA. (*Pause.*) I'm cold.

GEORGE. It's late.

MARTHA. Yes.

GEORGE. (*Long silence.*) It will be better.

MARTHA. (*Long silence.*) I don't . . . know.

GEORGE. It will be . . . maybe.

MARTHA. I'm . . . not . . . sure.

GEORGE. No.

MARTHA. Just . . . us?

GEORGE. Yes.

MARTHA. I don't suppose, maybe, we could . . .

GEORGE. No, Martha.

MARTHA. Yes. No.

GEORGE. Are you all right?

MARTHA. Yes. No.

GEORGE. (*Puts his hand gently on her shoulder; she puts her head back and he sings to her, very softly.*)

> Who's afraid of Virginia Woolf
> Virginia Woolf
> Virginia Woolf?

MARTHA. I . . . am . . . George. . . .

GEORGE. Who's afraid of Virginia Woolf. . . .

MARTHA. I . . . am . . . George. . . . I . . . am. . . . (*George nods, slowly. Silence; tableau.*)

CURTAIN

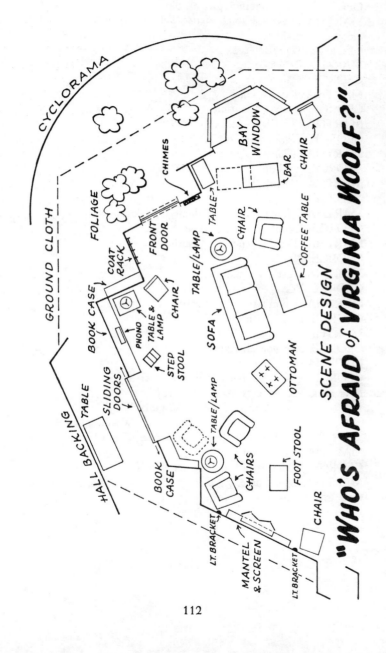

CYCLORAMA

GROUND CLOTH

HALL BACKING

TABLE

SLIDING DOORS

BOOK CASE

FOLIAGE

COAT RACK

FRONT DOOR

CHIMES

BAY WINDOW

BAR

CHAIR

PHONO

TABLE & LAMP

CHAIR

TABLE/LAMP

TABLE

CHAIR

STEP STOOL

SOFA

COFFEE TABLE

BOOK CASE

TABLE/LAMP

OTTOMAN

CHAIRS

FOOT STOOL

LT. BRACKET

MANTEL & SCREEN

LT. BRACKET

CHAIR

SCENE DESIGN

"WHO'S AFRAID of VIRGINIA WOOLF?"

PROPERTY PLOT

On bar:
  Ice bucket with ice cubes
  1 bottle gin (full)
  1 bottle bourbon (½ full)
  1 bottle brandy (enough for 2 drinks)
  1 "breakaway bottle"—new one each performance
  4 old-fashion glasses (1 with crushed ice)
  5 highball glasses
  1 water pitcher with water

Window seat:
  Several books, including blue one in u. section
  Newspaper on floor

Table L. of sofa:
  Ashtray
  Box of matches

Sofa:
  Sweater thrown over back L. end

Coffee table:
  Silver cup with cigarettes
  Matches—box
  1 old-fashion glass with water u. edge
  1 ashtray

U. L. corner book case:
  Phonograph (amplifier, turntable and speaker)
  Record jackets
  1 copy Beethoven's 7th
  1 copy "Working with the Miles Davis Quartet" 7th down in pile
  Catholic Missal L. of phone

Bookshelf u. R.:
  Book with marker, 5th shelf

Chair R.:
  1 book with marker and pencil on L. arm
  4 books on floor L.
  2 magazines on floor R.

113

Footstool
  2 newspapers
  2 books, top ot newspapers
  Newspaper, wrapped, leaning on D. edge
  Quarterly magazine on floor R.
  Book on top above

Chair D. R.:
  Folded newspaper

Mantel:
  Box with cigarettes C.
  Cigarette holder, D. of box
  Matches
  Clock, U. end, to read 2:05 at curtain, running
  Small picture D. end
  George's glasses in case D. of clock
  Glass (breakable) in fireplace
  Fire screen closed
  Ashtray D. of clock

Ottoman:
  1 book, open face up, R. end
  1 magazine (Saturday Review) on floor R.

Stepstool U. L. C.:
  1 book on top
  Door chimes, by front door

OFF STAGE:
Gun (George) (trick gun with Chinese parasol in barrel) R.
Extra ice (George) L.
Extra bottle bourbon, full with cork (George) L.
Extra bottle brandy, full with cork (George) L.
Extra bottle brandy, with peeled label and ¼ full (Honey) R.
1½ dozen snapdragons, mixed pink and white, tied with wire (George)
    L.
Extra glasses L.
1 package Pep-o-Mint life savers (Nick) L.
1 package Kent cigarettes (Nick) L.
Extra matches L.
Key ring with keys and small knife (George) L.
4 coats (all) L.
2 purses (small pillbox in Honey's) (Martha and Honey) L.
Wrist watch (George)

ACT ONE

INTERMISSION

Sponge up all water, check that matches are dry
Remove all but ice cubes from bucket
Move ottoman to Act I marks
Replace water in ashtray on coffee table
Move book with marker from floor to chair R.
Chest position of red chair C.
Make gin bottle ¾ full
Make brandy bottle ¼ full
Check front door closed
Move sliding doors to marks (L. 6" open, R. 12" closed)
Close in fire screen, check no glass showing, check floor for **glass**
Strike sweater from behind chair R.

ACT TWO

Refill ice bucket when George brings it off

INTERMISSION

Strike suit coat from coat rack
Check that there are 3 highball glasses on bar
Check that there is space for book on the shelf U. R.
Open front door
Sponge up water and check matches on coffee table
Take earrings from coffee table to dressing room (Martha)
Check that amplifier is off

NEW PLAYS

★ **HONOUR by Joanna Murray-Smith.** In a series of intense confrontations, a wife, husband, lover and daughter negotiate the forces of passion, history, responsibility and honour. "HONOUR makes for surprisingly interesting viewing. Tight, crackling dialogue (usually played out in punchy verbal duels) captures characters unable to deal with emotions ... Murray-Smith effectively places her characters in situations that strip away pretense." *–Variety* "... the play's virtues are strong: a distinctive theatrical voice, passionate concerns ... HONOUR might just capture a few honors of its own." *–Time Out Magazine* [1M, 3W] ISBN: 0-8222-1683-3

★ **MR. PETERS' CONNECTIONS by Arthur Miller.** Mr. Miller describes the protagonist as existing in a dream-like state when the mind is "freed to roam from real memories to conjectures, from trivialities to tragic insights, from terror of death to glorying in one's being alive." With this memory play, the Tony Award and Pulitzer Prize-winner reaffirms his stature as the world's foremost dramatist. "... a cross between Joycean stream-of-consciousness and Strindberg's dream plays, sweetened with a dose of William Saroyan's philosophical whimsy ... CONNECTIONS is most intriguing ..." *–The NY Times* [5M, 3W] ISBN: 0-8222-1687-6

★ **THE WAITING ROOM by Lisa Loomer.** Three women from different centuries meet in a doctor's waiting room in this dark comedy about the timeless quest for beauty – and its cost. "... THE WAITING ROOM ... is a bold, risky melange of conflicting elements that is ... terrifically moving ... There's no resisting the fierce emotional pull of the play." *–The NY Times* "... one of the high points of this year's Off-Broadway season ... THE WAITING ROOM is well worth a visit." *–Back Stage* [7M, 4W, flexible casting] ISBN: 0-8222-1594-2

★ **THE OLD SETTLER by John Henry Redwood.** A sweet-natured comedy about two church-going sisters in 1943 Harlem and the handsome young man who rents a room in their apartment. "For all of its decent sentiments, THE OLD SETTLER avoids sentimentality. It has the authenticity and lack of pretense of an Early American sampler." *–The NY Times* "We've had some fine plays Off-Broadway this season, and this is one of the best." *–The NY Post* [1M, 3W] ISBN: 0-8-222-1642-6

★ **LAST TRAIN TO NIBROC by Arlene Hutton.** In 1940 two young strangers share a seat on a train bound east only to find their paths will cross again. "All aboard. LAST TRAIN TO NIBROC is a sweetly told little chamber romance." *–Show Business* "... [a] gently charming little play, reminiscent of Thornton Wilder in its look at rustic Americans who are to be treasured for their simplicity and directness ..." *–Associated Press* "The old formula of boy wins girls, boy loses girl, boy wins girl still works ... [a] well-made play that perfectly captures a slice of small-town-life-gone-by." *–Back Stage* [1M, 1W] ISBN: 0-8222-1753-8

★ **OVER THE RIVER AND THROUGH THE WOODS by Joe DiPietro.** Nick sees both sets of his grandparents every Sunday for dinner. This is routine until he has to tell them that he's been offered a dream job in Seattle. The news doesn't sit so well. "A hilarious family comedy that is even funnier than his long running musical revue *I Love You, You're Perfect, Now Change.*" *–Back Stage* "Loaded with laughs every step of the way." *–Star-Ledger* [3M, 3W] ISBN: 0-8222-1712-0

★ **SIDE MAN by Warren Leight.** 1999 Tony Award winner. This is the story of a broken family and the decline of jazz as popular entertainment. "... a tender, deeply personal memory play about the turmoil in the family of a jazz musician as his career crumbles at the dawn of the age of rock-and-roll ..." *–The NY Times* "[SIDE MAN] is an elegy for two things – a lost world and a lost love. When the two notes sound together in harmony, it is moving and graceful ..." *–The NY Daily News* "An atmospheric memory play ... with crisp dialogue and clearly drawn characters ... reflects the passing of an era with persuasive insight ... The joy and despair of the musicians is skillfully illustrated." *–Variety* [5M, 3W] ISBN: 0-8222-1721-X

DRAMATISTS PLAY SERVICE, INC.
440 Park Avenue South, New York, NY 10016 212-683-8960 Fax 212-213-1539
postmaster@dramatists.com www.dramatists.com

NEW PLAYS

★ **CLOSER by Patrick Marber.** Winner of the 1998 Olivier Award for Best Play and the 1999 New York Drama Critics Circle Award for Best Foreign Play. Four lives intertwine over the course of four and a half years in this densely plotted, stinging look at modern love and betrayal. "CLOSER is a sad, savvy, often funny play that casts a steely, unblinking gaze at the world of relationships and lets you come to your own conclusions … CLOSER does not merely hold your attention; it burrows into you." –*New York Magazine* "A powerful, darkly funny play about the cosmic collision between the sun of love and the comet of desire." –*Newsweek Magazine* [2M, 2W] ISBN: 0-8222-1722-8

★ **THE MOST FABULOUS STORY EVER TOLD by Paul Rudnick.** A stage manager, headset and prompt book at hand, brings the house lights to half, then dark, and cues the creation of the world. Throughout the play, she's in control of everything. In other words, she's either God, or she thinks she is. "Line by line, Mr. Rudnick may be the funniest writer for the stage in the United States today … One-liners, epigrams, withering put-downs and flashing repartee: These are the candles that Mr. Rudnick lights instead of cursing the darkness … a testament to the virtues of laughing … and in laughter, there is something like the memory of Eden." –*The NY Times* "Funny it is … consistently, rapaciously, deliriously … easily the funniest play in town." –*Variety* [4M, 5W] ISBN: 0-8222-1720-1

★ **A DOLL'S HOUSE by Henrik Ibsen, adapted by Frank McGuinness.** Winner of the 1997 Tony Award for Best Revival. "New, raw, gut-twisting and gripping. Easily the hottest drama this season." –*USA Today* "Bold, brilliant and alive." –*The Wall Street Journal* "A thunderclap of an evening that takes your breath away." –*Time Magazine* [4M, 4W, 2 boys] ISBN: 0-8222-1636-1

★ **THE HERBAL BED by Peter Whelan.** The play is based on actual events which occurred in Stratford-upon-Avon in the summer of 1613, when William Shakespeare's elder daughter was publicly accused of having a sexual liaison with a married neighbor and family friend. "In his probing new play, THE HERBAL BED … Peter Whelan muses about a sidelong event in the life of Shakespeare's family and creates a finely textured tapestry of love and lies in the early 17th-century Stratford." –*The NY Times* "It is a first rate drama with interesting moral issues of truth and expediency." –*The NY Post* [5M, 3W] ISBN: 0-8222-1675-2

★ **SNAKEBIT by David Marshall Grant.** A study of modern friendship when put to the test. "… a rather smart and absorbing evening of water-cooler theater, the intimate sort of Off-Broadway experience that has you picking apart the recognizable characters long after the curtain calls." – *The NY Times* "Off-Broadway keeps on presenting us with compelling reasons for going to the theater. The latest is SNAKEBIT, David Marshall Grant's smart new comic drama about being thirtysomething and losing one's way in life." –*The NY Daily News* [3M, 1W] ISBN: 0-8222-1724-4

★ **A QUESTION OF MERCY by David Rabe.** The Obie Award-winning playwright probes the sensitive and controversial issue of doctor-assisted suicide in the age of AIDS in this poignant drama. "There are many devastating ironies in Mr. Rabe's beautifully considered, piercingly clear-eyed work …" –*The NY Times* "With unsettling candor and disturbing insight, the play arouses pity and understanding of a troubling subject … Rabe's provocative tale is an affirmation of dignity that rings clear and true." –*Variety* [6M, 1W] ISBN: 0-8222-1643-4

★ **DIMLY PERCEIVED THREATS TO THE SYSTEM by Jon Klein.** Reality and fantasy overlap with hilarious results as this unforgettable family attempts to survive the nineties. "Here's a play whose point about fractured families goes to the heart, mind – and ears." –*The Washington Post* "… an end-of-the millennium comedy about a family on the verge of a nervous breakdown … Trenchant and hilarious …" –*The Baltimore Sun* [2M, 4W] ISBN: 0-8222-1677-9

DRAMATISTS PLAY SERVICE, INC.
440 Park Avenue South, New York, NY 10016 212-683-8960 Fax 212-213-1539
postmaster@dramatists.com   www.dramatists.com

NEW PLAYS

★ **AS BEES IN HONEY DROWN by Douglas Carter Beane.** Winner of the John Gassner Playwriting Award. A hot young novelist finds the subject of his new screenplay in a New York socialite who leads him into the world of *Auntie Mame* and *Breakfast at Tiffany's*, before she takes him for a ride. "A delicious soufflé of a satire ... [an] extremely entertaining fable for an age that always chooses image over substance." *–The NY Times* "... A witty assessment of one of the most active and relentless industries in a consumer society ... the creation of 'hot' young things, which the media have learned to mass produce with efficiency and zeal." *–The NY Daily News* [3M, 3W, flexible casting] ISBN: 0-8222-1651-5

★ **STUPID KIDS by John C. Russell.** In rapid, highly stylized scenes, the story follows four high-school students as they make their way from first through eighth period and beyond, struggling with the fears, frustrations, and longings peculiar to youth. "In STUPID KIDS ... playwright John C. Russell gets the opera of adolescence to a T ... The stylized teenspeak of STUPID KIDS ... suggests that Mr. Russell may have hidden a tape recorder under a desk in study hall somewhere and then scoured the tapes for good quotations ... it is the kids' insular, ceaselessly churning world, a pre-adult world of Doritos and libidos, that the playwright seeks to lay bare." *–The NY Times* "STUPID KIDS [is] a sharp-edged ... whoosh of teen angst and conformity anguish. It is also very funny." *–NY Newsday* [2M, 2W] ISBN: 0-8222-1698-1

★ **COLLECTED STORIES by Donald Margulies.** From Obie Award-winner Donald Margulies comes a provocative analysis of a student-teacher relationship that turns sour when the protégé becomes a rival. "With his fine ear for detail, Margulies creates an authentic, insular world, and he gives equal weight to the opposing viewpoints of two formidable characters." *–The LA Times* "This is probably Margulies' best play to date ..." *–The NY Post* "... always fluid and lively, the play is thick with ideas, like a stock-pot of good stew." *–The Village Voice* [2W] ISBN: 0-8222-1640-X

★ **FREEDOMLAND by Amy Freed.** An overdue showdown between a son and his father sets off fireworks that illuminate the neurosis, rage and anxiety of one family – and of America at the turn of the millennium. "FREEDOMLAND's more obvious links are to *Buried Child* and *Bosoms and Neglect*. Freed, like Guare, is an inspired wordsmith with a gift for surreal touches in situations grounded in familiar and real territory." *–Curtain Up* [3M, 4W] ISBN: 0-8222-1719-8

★ **STOP KISS by Diana Son.** A poignant and funny play about the ways, both sudden and slow, that lives can change irrevocably. "There's so much that is vital and exciting about STOP KISS ... you want to embrace this young author and cheer her onto other works ... the writing on display here is funny and credible ... you also will be charmed by its heartfelt characters and up-to-the-minute humor." *–The NY Daily News* "... irresistibly exciting ... a sweet, sad, and enchantingly sincere play." *–The NY Times* [3M, 3W] ISBN: 0-8222-1731-7

★ **THREE DAYS OF RAIN by Richard Greenberg.** The sins of fathers and mothers make for a bittersweet elegy in this poignant and revealing drama. "... a work so perfectly judged it heralds the arrival of a major playwright ... Greenberg is extraordinary." *–The NY Daily News* "Greenberg's play is filled with graceful passages that are by turns melancholy, harrowing, and often, quite funny." *–Variety* [2M, 1W] ISBN: 0-8222-1676-0

★ **THE WEIR by Conor McPherson.** In a bar in rural Ireland, the local men swap spooky stories in an attempt to impress a young woman from Dublin who recently moved into a nearby "haunted" house. However, the tables are soon turned when she spins a yarn of her own. "You shed all sense of time at this beautiful and devious new play." *–The NY Times* "Sheer theatrical magic. I have rarely been so convinced that I have just seen a modern classic. Tremendous." *–The London Daily Telegraph* [4M, 1W] ISBN: 0-8222-1706-6

DRAMATISTS PLAY SERVICE, INC.
440 Park Avenue South, New York, NY 10016 212-683-8960 Fax 212-213-1539
postmaster@dramatists.com www.dramatists.com